Ouya Unity Game Development

Your guide to building interactive media-rich 3D games with Ouya

Gary Riches

PUBLISHING
BIRMINGHAM - MUMBAI

Ouya Unity Game Development

Copyright © 2013 Packt Publishing

All rights reserved. No part of this book may be reproduced, stored in a retrieval system, or transmitted in any form or by any means, without the prior written permission of the publisher, except in the case of brief quotations embedded in critical articles or reviews.

Every effort has been made in the preparation of this book to ensure the accuracy of the information presented. However, the information contained in this book is sold without warranty, either express or implied. Neither the author, nor Packt Publishing, and its dealers and distributors will be held liable for any damages caused or alleged to be caused directly or indirectly by this book.

Packt Publishing has endeavored to provide trademark information about all of the companies and products mentioned in this book by the appropriate use of capitals. However, Packt Publishing cannot guarantee the accuracy of this information.

First published: October 2013

Production Reference: 1171013

Published by Packt Publishing Ltd.
Livery Place
35 Livery Street
Birmingham B3 2PB, UK.

ISBN 978-1-78355-970-1

www.packtpub.com

Cover Image by Jarek Blaminsky (milak6@wp.pl)

Credits

Author
Gary Riches

Reviewers
John P. Doran
Steve Jarman

Acquisition Editor
Kevin Colaco

Commissioning Editor
Sharvari Tawde

Technical Editors
Novina Kewalramani
Amit Shetty

Project Coordinator
Amigya Khurana

Proofreader
Lesley Harrison

Indexer
Mariammal Chettiyar

Production Coordinator
Kyle Albuquerque

Cover Work
Kyle Albuquerque

About the Author

Gary Riches is a longstanding member of the iOS developer community. He has a keen interest not only in established sections of the industry such as gaming but also in emerging technologies such as Ouya, GameStick, and others.

Filled with a passion to program on new systems, he has just become a registered Wii U developer and will also create content for Xbox One and PlayStation 4. To target so many platforms he uses Unity, which he learned while working on the Augmented Reality SBook for Saddington Baynes.

When not building software for other companies, he builds his own business by creating photo manipulation apps such as Zombify Me, games such as Aztec Antics and Amazed, and also works on educational apps and games such as Nursery Rhymes: Volume 1, 2, and 3.

Acknowledgment

I would very much like to thank my wonderful wife, Sophie. Without her support and enthusiasm I would not be where I am today or the man I am today. This one paragraph cannot thank her enough but I doubt Packt Publishing will let me write a book to her so it'll have to do. I must also thank my beautiful daughter Evie, she provides a brilliant distraction when I'm taking a break or thinking of what to write or do next.

I must also thank my Mum and Dad, they provided me with computer equipment from an early age, without which I would have never been able to learn how to program. Along with the rest of my family, my brother David, helped to foster a very strong interest in computers and computing. I will never forget when he made our Spectrum flash insults at me on the screen by programming it and it seemed like pure magic.

Dave Mark and Jeff LaMarche wrote the book I learnt iOS development from and without them I would have missed the mobile train completely.

And finally I must thank all of those from the #actionscript IRC channel where I first learned to program. Special thanks goes out to Rob Gibson, Mark Griffin, Glenn Jones, Andreas Rønning, and all the other people from that channel that I haven't mentioned.

About the Reviewers

John P. Doran is a technical game designer who has worked on all manners of educational, mod, and professional game projects. He graduated from DigiPen Institute of Technology in Redmond, WA with a Bachelor of Science in Game Design.

He previously worked at LucasArts in San Francisco, CA on Star Wars 1313 as an intern Level Designer. He is currently the lead instructor of the DigiPen-Ubisoft Campus Game Programming Program, instructing graduate level students in an intensive, advanced-level game programming curriculum. He's also a Software Engineer at DigiPen's Singapore campus teaching advanced usage of C/C++, UDK, Flash, Unity, and ActionScript in a development environment to students.

He is the author of *Mastering UDK Game Development*, *Getting Started with UDK*, and the co-writer of *UDK iOS Game Development Beginner's Guide*, all available from *Packt Publishing*.

You can check his blog at http://johnpdoran.com and contact him at john@johnpdoran.com.

> Thanks so much to the author for allowing me to give him my thoughts while writing the book, I hope that they helped.
>
> I'd also like to thank my brother, Chris Doran, and my wife Hannah Mai for being there for me whenever I need it and being patient while I was working on this. I'd also like to thank all the lovely people at Packt Publishing for all of their support and know-how!

Steve Jarman is a software developer from Sydney, Australia. He has been programming for almost 30 years; starting out on a Commodore 64 at an early age. Since 2008, Steve's efforts have been focused on video game development, primarily using the Unity engine. He is the creator of several successful mobile apps and games. Steve can be contacted through his website at www.stevejarman.com.

www.PacktPub.com

Support files, eBooks, discount offers and more

You might want to visit www.PacktPub.com for support files and downloads related to your book.

Did you know that Packt offers eBook versions of every book published, with PDF and ePub files available? You can upgrade to the eBook version at www.PacktPub.com and as a print book customer, you are entitled to a discount on the eBook copy. Get in touch with us at service@packtpub.com for more details.

At www.PacktPub.com, you can also read a collection of free technical articles, sign up for a range of free newsletters and receive exclusive discounts and offers on Packt books and eBooks.

http://PacktLib.PacktPub.com

Do you need instant solutions to your IT questions? PacktLib is Packt's online digital book library. Here, you can access, read and search across Packt's entire library of books.

Why Subscribe?

- Fully searchable across every book published by Packt
- Copy and paste, print and bookmark content
- On demand and accessible via web browser

Free Access for Packt account holders

If you have an account with Packt at www.PacktPub.com, you can use this to access PacktLib today and view nine entirely free books. Simply use your login credentials for immediate access.

Table of Contents

Preface	**1**
Chapter 1: What Is Ouya and Why Does It Matter?	**5**
The early years	5
The crash	6
The recovery	6
Home computers	7
Advancement of game consoles	9
The first indie console	9
Cellular games	10
The iPhone	10
The competitors	11
Current day situation	12
History of Ouya	12
Ouya's release	13
Summary	13
Chapter 2: Setting Up Unity and the Ouya Plugin	**15**
Installing the Android SDK	15
Installing Java	16
Setting up the Android SDK	16
Setting up the Android NDK	17
Connecting Ouya to your Windows computer	18
Connecting Ouya to your Mac computer	20
Ouya Development Kit	21
The Unity project	22
The bundle identifier	23
Setting up Ouya Panel	24

Ouya required prefabs	26
Building, running, and compiling an application	26
Summary	**27**
Chapter 3: Setting Up Your Game	**29**
Boo, C#, or UnityScript	29
Boo	29
UnityScript	30
C#	30
The project structure	30
Setting up your Scenes	32
Scripts and MonoDevelop	33
Scene progression	36
The title screen menu	36
Advancing to the game	37
Ouya controller support	38
Creating the level	41
Prefabs	41
Creating a Prefab	41
Materials	42
Multidimensional arrays	42
The BuildLevel method	44
Summary	**47**
Chapter 4: Adding a Character and Making Them Move	**49**
Making the camera move	49
Making the character move	52
Ouya controller support	59
Animating the character	60
Summary	**63**
Chapter 5: Adding Finesse to Your Game	**65**
Texturing your Prefabs	65
Adding a background	68
Adding extra levels	70
Level complete detection	72
Moving to the next level	73
Restarting our level	74
Adding sounds	74
Summary	**76**

Chapter 6: Show Me the Money! — 77
Setting up your purchase — 77
Setting up your game — 78
Implementing the Ouya payment framework — 79
How to manage your purchases — 80
Getting the list of products — 81
Limiting your levels — 82
Unlocking levels for people who have paid — 83
Buying your product — 84
Adding a new menu item — 84
The buy method — 85
Hiding menu items — 87
Submitting your game — 87
Summary — 88
Chapter 7: Building Cross-platform Games — 89
Platform Dependent Compilation — 90
Changing the TitleScreen scene — 91
Removing In-App Purchases — 93
Mobile controls — 94
Summary — 97
Index — 99

Preface

As the Ouya technology is so new, finding information about developing for it can be hard. This book covers all that you'll need to know to create your game and add great features to it, such as controller functionality, animation, sounds, and monetization. We'll even show you how to make it work on Android phones and tablets.

What this book covers

Chapter 1, *What is Ouya and Why Does It Matter?*, gives a brief history of video games. We'll show where they've come from, where they're going, and how the Ouya technology fits in to that journey.

Chapter 2, *Setting Up Unity and the Ouya Plugin*, will guide you through installing the development kits needed and show how to set up your Unity project so that you can build to the Ouya platform.

Chapter 3, *Setting Up Your Game*, explains the differences between three of the languages you can use to program in Unity and builds the foundation for our game.

Chapter 4, *Adding a Character and Making Them Move*, explains about adding movement to the camera and making it follow a player around the level. It also explains expanding upon your character and adding animations.

Chapter 5, *Adding Finesse to Your Game*, explains how to texture your prefabs, add sounds and more levels. This chapter will really flesh out the game.

Chapter 6, *Show Me the Money!*, will add In-App Purchases, which will allow you to monetize your awesome new creations.

Chapter 7, *Building Cross-platform Games*, explains that one of Unity's strongest features is its write-once, publish-everywhere functionality. Leverage this ability and get your game running on Android phones and tablets.

Preface

What you need for this book

For this book you will be required to download the free version of Unity available at the following link:

- `http://www.unity3d.com/unity/download`

Your computer should also meet the minimum requirements, as stated on the Unity website. For the latest requirements, refer to the following link:

- `http://unity3d.com/unity/system-requirements`

You will also need the Android SDK, NDK, Java, and Ouya Development Kit. The download, installation, and setup of these is covered in *Chapter 2, Setting Up Unity and the Ouya Plugin*.

Who this book is for

This book is for beginner programmers upwards; a basic understanding of Unity is required. All concepts are explained, even if they are simple.

Conventions

In this book, you will find a number of styles of text that distinguish between different kinds of information. Here are some examples of these styles, and an explanation of their meaning.

Code words in text are shown as follows: "We won't be using the `System.Collections` in this script, so we can go ahead and delete that line although it won't affect if you leave it in".

A block of code is set as follows:

```
usingUnityEngine;

public class AdvanceToNextLevel : MonoBehaviour {

  // Use this for initialization
  void Awake () {
    Application.LoadLevel("TitleScreen");
  }
}
```

New terms and **important words** are shown in bold. Words that you see on the screen, in menus or dialog boxes for example, appear in the text like this: "We're going to create some new folders to hold other files in project, so click on the **Create** drop-down menu, which is located just underneath the **Project** tab in panel you opened".

> Warnings or important notes appear in a box like this.

> Tips and tricks appear like this.

Reader feedback

Feedback from our readers is always welcome. Let us know what you think about this book—what you liked or may have disliked. Reader feedback is important for us to develop titles that you really get the most out of.

To send us general feedback, simply send an e-mail to feedback@packtpub.com, and mention the book title via the subject of your message.

If there is a topic that you have expertise in and you are interested in either writing or contributing to a book, see our author guide on www.packtpub.com/authors.

Customer support

Now that you are the proud owner of a Packt book, we have a number of things to help you to get the most from your purchase.

Downloading the example code

You can download the example code files for all Packt books you have purchased from your account at http://www.packtpub.com. If you purchased this book elsewhere, you can visit http://www.packtpub.com/support and register to have the files e-mailed directly to you.

Errata

Although we have taken every care to ensure the accuracy of our content, mistakes do happen. If you find a mistake in one of our books—maybe a mistake in the text or the code—we would be grateful if you would report this to us. By doing so, you can save other readers from frustration and help us improve subsequent versions of this book. If you find any errata, please report them by visiting http://www.packtpub.com/submit-errata, selecting your book, clicking on the **errata submission form** link, and entering the details of your errata. Once your errata are verified, your submission will be accepted and the errata will be uploaded on our website, or added to any list of existing errata, under the Errata section of that title. Any existing errata can be viewed by selecting your title from http://www.packtpub.com/support.

Piracy

Piracy of copyright material on the Internet is an ongoing problem across all media. At Packt, we take the protection of our copyright and licenses very seriously. If you come across any illegal copies of our works, in any form, on the Internet, please provide us with the location address or website name immediately so that we can pursue a remedy.

Please contact us at copyright@packtpub.com with a link to the suspected pirated material.

We appreciate your help in protecting our authors, and our ability to bring you valuable content.

Questions

You can contact us at questions@packtpub.com if you are having a problem with any aspect of the book, and we will do our best to address it.

What Is Ouya and Why Does It Matter?

Video games! From the bedroom developer to the video-game company, we can all create games that can inspire, educate, or are just plain fun. Let's look how video games got where they are and the history of indie game development till the current day with the Ouya.

The early years

It started on January 25, 1947. The United States Patent and Trademark office received a request for a patent on an invention described as a cathode ray amusement device. The patent was granted on December 14, 1948 and, while it was never marketed or sold to the general public, it was truly one of the first video games. The machine was a crude electromechanical device that did not use any memory or programming.

In the early 1950s, simple computer programs started to surface but they lacked interactivity, and with the limited accessibility of computers they would not be seen by many and were destined to be forgotten.

It wasn't until the 1970s that arcade machines as we know them came about. Nolan Bushnell and Ted Dabney created a coin-operated game named **Computer Space**. Nutting Associates bought the game and produced over 1,500 arcade machines. Computer Space had a steep learning curve, and because of this was unsuccessful, but it must still be remembered for being the first mass-produced video game offered for general sale.

Bushnell and Dabney went on to establish **Atari** in 1972 and assigned one of their employees, Allen Alcorn, with a training exercise. During that exercise, he created **Pong**, the virtual table tennis game we all know and love. Bushnell and Dabney were impressed with Alcorn's work and they decided to manufacture the game. Overall, Atari sold approximately 19,000 pong machines.

Creating a machine that could play a game was all well and good, but innovators were looking towards the future. What if a machine could play multiple games? This would truly give it the edge over its single-game relatives. Ralph Baer had begun work on such a machine in the late 1960s. He was demoing it in the early 1970s to companies including Sylvania, Sears, Magnavox, and General Electric. Magnavox licensed the system and produced the first video-game console in the world, the **Magnavox Odyssey** console. This console used cartridges containing jumpers that would alter the circuitry logic of the machine. A multigame device coupled with a strong marketing push meant that Magnavox sold over 100,000 Odyssey consoles in their first year. Over the lifetime of the console, the Odyssey console sold over 2,000,000 units.

The crash

By 1977, the market was flooded with cheap clones of Pong. Due to the sheer amount of cloned devices, none saw sustainable sales. Companies, faced with obsolete and aging stock, started to sell their systems at a loss causing a crash in the price of the devices and leading to many companies pulling out of the games market. Only two were able to weather the storm, Atari and Magnavox, but both reported losses in 1977 and 1978.

However, in 1978 a new game, **Space Invaders**, was released by a company named Taito. The game was a huge commercial success allowing Taito to create a US office and paving the way for a renaissance in video games. Atari licensed Space Invaders for their new machine, **Atari 2600**. This console revived the home video-game market, backed by the success of Space Invaders.

The recovery

While the Magnavox Odyssey console could play multiple games, the software was embedded on chips in the console; the cartridges would simply modify the circuitry inside the console with jumpers. The configuration of the jumpers would define which game you played. This meant that no software changes could occur on the device but hardware changes only. If a new game was created you'd have to buy a new device to attach to your television.

A new breed of console had been conceived and was starting to arrive, one that would allow new circuitry to be added easily and allow new games to be played without the need to buy a new machine. The trick was to have microprocessors inside the video-game cartridge. When the cartridge was plugged in to the device, it became part of the console, running whatever program was stored in **Read Only Memory (ROM)** on the cartridge.

While the system for running games had improved, video-game production itself was still very basic with most development being carried out by one person. They would create the concept, write the code, draw the graphics, and make the sound, much like one-man developer teams.

In 1979, four developers from Atari realized that the games they had created for meager pay were earning Atari around $60,000,000 a year. They decided to leave and set up their own company. **Activision**, the first third-party developer was founded.

After the success of Space Invaders, video games started to become mainstream. Arcade machines entered shopping malls, restaurants, and convenience stores bringing about an explosion in video-game usage. Space Invaders sold over 360,000 arcade machines worldwide and generated over $2,000,000,000 in quarters. From 1978 to 1981, the sales of arcade machines went from $50,000,000 to $900,000,000.

By 1982, video games generated more revenue than both pop music and Hollywood films combined.

It was around this time that a debt-ridden toy company named Nintendo turned around its fortunes, by firstly, securing the rights to distribute the Magnavox Odyssey console in Japan and secondly, creating their own games for arcades and on the Atari 2600 machine, Intellivision, and ColecoVision video-game systems. In 1985, Nintendo released **Nintendo Entertainment System (NES)** and the system was a huge success.

Home computers

Alongside the video-game consoles, home computers started to arrive on the scene. Notable entrants were the **Commodore 64**, the **Sinclair ZX Spectrum**, the **BBC Micro**, and the **Acorn Electron** machines. These machines allowed their operators to program their own software. Magazines would print reams of code, to be hand typed to produce a game. There were mailing lists and, at some locations, even local shops selling a programmer's wares on their shelves in the form of floppy discs, tapes, or cartridges.

By 1984, computer gaming had overtaken the console gaming market. While not as simple to use, the ability to create programs for them was appealing and the software was more readily available.

The Commodore 64 machine was launched in 1982 and shipped with a **Beginners' All-purpose Symbolic Instruction Code (BASIC)** programming environment. This spawned a generation of bedroom programmers. They would work on software to show off their coding prowess, which could achieve the most impressive effects within the memory constraints of the machine, and are largely credited for creating the demo scene as it is today.

In 1985, the **Atari ST** and the **Commodore Amiga** machines arrived. While expensive initially, these machines became more affordable within a few years. The power of home computers was coming on in leaps and bounds, and both computers excelled in certain areas.

Home computers were ahead of contemporary game consoles in terms of graphical performance. The Amiga machine had many hardware revisions and the PC was improving with dedicated graphics and sound cards.

None of the game consoles allowed any hobbyist development, they all were closed systems. If you wanted to program, you would need to get a computer and learn how to code for it.

It was around this time that many small game companies were founded in the UK; Bitmap Brothers, Psygnosis, and Team 17 to name a few. While these companies started off small, the success of their games led to rapid expansion. While some have now ceased to exist and others have been bought out by larger companies, games based on their intellectual property and franchises still exist and are available for sale today. Some of the Bitmap Brothers games are available on Xbox Live Arcade, and Sony has just announced a remake of **Shadow of the Beast**, an early game from Psygnosis.

Advancement of game consoles

In 1995, the **PlayStation** console was launched. The hype around the launch and the fact that the machine could produce incredible 3D graphics for the time and output CD quality music meant the console was an instant success. Whereas developers for the PC would have to worry about hardware fragmentation, with the PlayStation all consoles had a standard set of specifications. There was a vibrant console modification scene that set about getting the PlayStation to run programs it wasn't intended to via **chipping**, a process that involved soldering chips on to the main PlayStation circuit board to circumvent its copy protection schemes. While Sony tried to clamp down on console modification by releasing new hardware revisions, they also acknowledged that there was a real desire to program for their machine.

The first indie console

In 1997, Sony made a new console available, the **Net Yaroze** console. A Net Yaroze console purchase included an **Software Development Kit (SDK)**, a cable to connect it to your PC and some documentation. You would also have access to an online community of other Net Yaroze programmers. No other console manufacturer had offered such a device before. It wasn't a full development kit, but it would allow any member of the public to purchase one via mail order and start creating games. The Official PlayStation Magazine guide would regularly feature demos that had been created by Net Yaroze enthusiasts. A few of them were made into commercial PlayStation games and one game, Time Slip, was even updated and released on Xbox Live Arcade in 2012.

This kind of console manufacturer interaction with the enthusiast developer community was not repeated with PlayStation 2 or PlayStation 3 by Sony, or the Xbox or Xbox 360 by Microsoft. While they offer indie developer programs, they were often relegated to deep menu sections and poorly publicized over their more elaborately produced arcade games.

By the time these later consoles were established, the cost of games' development had sky-rocketed, a result of the complexity needed in modern games and the graphical detail could now be displayed. For example, **Grand Theft Auto IV** which was released on PlayStation 3, Xbox 360, and PC had over 150 developers working on it and cost more than $100,000,000 to produce. A far cry from the one man teams of the late 1970s and early 1980s.

Cellular games

While consoles and computers were well established, cell phones were still quite basic in comparison. In 1998, you would be happy with a Nokia phone that could display two colors. A brand new game was now coming installed on every new Nokia phone, **Snake**!. The game was simple but it was played by a massive audience as there were few alternatives. In 2003, with the success of Nintendo's **Game Boy** line of handheld consoles, Nokia tried to capitalize on cellular gaming and released the **N-Gage** game. The N-Gage game was not well received by the press or general public, but Nokia persisted with the idea until 2005 before relegating the N-Gage brand to a software service that was to slowly die.

Meanwhile, Microsoft had been producing **Windows Mobile** for cell phones. These devices offered true multitasking, the software you could purchase online and install from an SD card, advanced calendar syncing, and document viewing among other features. Many of them also offered resistive touch screens. Unfortunately, the complexity of the devices and a poor user experience hampered general uptake of the devices.

Cellular development was not in a good position. There were myriad processor speeds, screen sizes, memory amounts, and phone abilities. Any development, usually in Java for Nokia's Symbian platform, had to cater for the lowest common denominator, meaning game development was not being pushed forward on cellular devices.

The iPhone

This was about to change. On June 29, 2007 Apple released the **iPhone** device. This device was far ahead of all its competitors at the time. The iPhone device supported multitouch, capacitive screens which allowed more accuracy, and new types of gestures that hadn't been seen before, such as pinching a screen to zoom in or out. Apple's attention to user experience was evident throughout the device. Scrolling and animations were executed with a fluidity not previously seen in a cell phone. Shortly after, the **iPod Touch** device was released. It used the same operating system and had the recognisability of the already ubiquitous iPod name. Like the PlayStation before it, there was suddenly a very popular device with only one hardware configuration. Developers were very quick to try and find a way to create software for the device. Apple, responding to developers while hesitant to open up their platform to third parties, provided documentation and help on how to build **HTML 5** apps for their device. These apps, as Apple called them, couldn't offer a full range of functionality as they were unable to access much of the hardware on the iPhone.

Things went on that way for a year but Apple had been working in the background. They had created a new phone, the **iPhone 3G** phone, and a new version of the iPhone OS to run on it. There were multiple new features, but most revolutionary was the **App Store** feature. Released on June 10, 2008, the App Store feature promised a store front for everyone's apps, all on an equal footing. Apple would handle all the financial transactions and the file hosting, and take a 30 percent cut. This is now what most app stores offer but the amount given to a developer prior to this was considerably less.

While the phones were quite powerful, a user's expectations of what a handheld game was hadn't been defined yet. If you were upgrading from Snake then these were absolute power houses, but as they were handheld devices no one expected Grand Theft Auto on them. It meant that developers were free to experiment with all types of games. It enabled bedroom development again. One developer with a computer and an iPhone was able to create a game to their specification and could have it on sale alongside titles from Sega, EA, Square Enix and other large, professional game companies.

The competitors

Not wanting to miss out on the new cellular gold rush, Google announced its Android operating system in 2007 and the first Android phone was released in October 2008. Android's unique selling point was its openness. While Apple was allowing third-party development for its iPhone and iPod touch devices, the developers were restricted in what their apps could do. Apple provided access to high level methods in iPhone OS while Android allowed almost any aspect of the operating system to be modified or augmented as the developer saw fit.

Android was essentially free for any cell phone manufacturers to install on their devices, so uptake of Android grew massively. Some just installed a basic, unmodified version of Android while others, such as Samsung and HTC, installed their own version of Android for better or worse. Others, such as Amazon, have taken Android, forked, and modified it beyond all recognition. That's the beauty and flaw of Android, you have the ability to do whatever you want with the operating system. Sometimes the results are stunning but other times the results are a disaster. This is what Apple is trying to avoid by limiting software access and producing their own hardware.

Current day situation

As of writing this text, it's 2013 now, and while indie games are big business they can still be created by small teams. The large publishers have invaded the app stores and are doing what they do best, making money by releasing already established IP and buying anyone who does well, but the smaller teams are competing and in some cases outdoing the larger companies. **Minecraft**, a game initially created by one man, has pulled in over $80,000,000, and **Angry Birds**, created by Rovio with a team of twelve developers, has made over $100,000,000.

If you are lucky enough to create a successful app you'll earn very good money, but the pool to be selected from has grown massively since 2008. There are now an estimated 900,000 apps on the app store for iOS alone with a similar amount for Android.

History of Ouya

On June 10, 2012 a new kind of game console was imagined. With its support for four controllers and output to the TV, it was to try and capture the glory days of console gaming; you and your friends sitting on a sofa together, having fun playing games. It used a crowd-funding website named **Kickstarter** to announce itself and generate funds. The **Ouya** development team was asking for $950,000. Backers would receive access to the device when it was released. The Kickstarter fund-raising goal was raised within 8 hours. Ouya holds the record for the best first day performance of any project on Kickstarter to date. Ouya became the most quickly funded project on Kickstarter to reach one million dollars, and went on to become the eighth project in Kickstarter history to raise more than a million dollars. At the end of the funding, the development team had received $8,596,474. The cost of the device was $99 and it ran Android. This meant there was a large library of games available to easily port across to Ouya. Developers heavily backed the Ouya as the consistent hardware specification is a boon to Android developers who normally have to contend with device specification fragmentation.

Ouya's release

Suddenly the Ouya is in the world's press. Events are unfolding very similar to the iPhone release and developers want to get in to the Ouya development while it's still fresh and new.

While it runs Android, it's a complete visual change. Special consideration needs to be taken to implement the controller support and in-app purchase. All games on the Ouya need to offer a demo version or be free. The games are monetized by creating unlockable content that can be enabled via an in-app purchase.

The Ouya already has a some good games, but there is plenty of space for new ideas to make their mark. Some of the current games are exclusive to the platform, some of them are ports from large publishers, such as **Square Enix**, but all of them receive equal footing on the Ouya, yours will too.

It's all new territory again and anything can be a success!

Summary

There are parallels between the early days of the video-game industry and where indie game development is now. While it had mostly been viewed as a niche area previously, Sony, Microsoft, and Nintendo are all embracing indie developers for the next generation, and there is huge interest in the market now. We're here as we want to capitalize on the current interest for indie development. In *Chapter 2, Setting Up Unity and the Ouya Plugin*, we're going to go through the steps required to set up **Unity** for Ouya development.

2
Setting Up Unity and the Ouya Plugin

In this chapter, you'll be guided through installing the Android SDK, **Android NDK** (**Native Development Kit**), **Java**, **Java JDK** (**Java Development Kit**), and **ODK** (**Ouya Development Kit**) and shown how to set up your **Unity** project so that you can build Ouya. Once this is complete we'll be ready to start our game, **Sokoban**. Sokoban is a classic crate-moving game where the player has to get all the crates in a warehouse on to their designated goal tiles. Sokoban in Japanese roughly translates to warehouse keeper.

 These instructions have been written for Windows but the installation of the SDK, Java, NDK, and ODK will be similar. Where the process differs greatly we'll include some extra information.

Installing the Android SDK

It may not look like it, but Ouya runs Android so we'll need to install the Android SDK. This is going to allow us to compile from Unity and then add the game to the our Ouya or Android device. Go to `http://developer.android.com/sdk/index.html` in your browser and you'll see a large, blue button on the right that says **Download the SDK** followed by **ADT Bundle for Windows**.

Press the large, blue button and you'll be presented with a **Terms and Conditions** page and a radio button asking whether you want the **32-bit** or **64-bit** version. We're going to go with the 32-bit version for this book. Once downloaded, install it on your machine. For the purposes of this book, I'm going to install it to `c:\adt-bundle-windows-x86-20130729`.

Setting Up Unity and the Ouya Plugin

Installing Java

Next you'll need to install Java for your computer. Go to `http://www.java.com/en/download/ie_manual.jsp?locale=en` in your browser and click on the red button that says **Agree and Start Free Download**. Download and install the file.

>  Be sure to uncheck the boxes where Oracle attempts to get you to install toolbars and other bloatware.

Setting up the Android SDK

Once Java is installed you'll be able to configure your Android SDK. Navigate to the folder where you have installed the Android SDK and you'll see an application called **SDK Manager** that has the Android mascot as its icon. Open the SDK Manager and you'll see something like this:

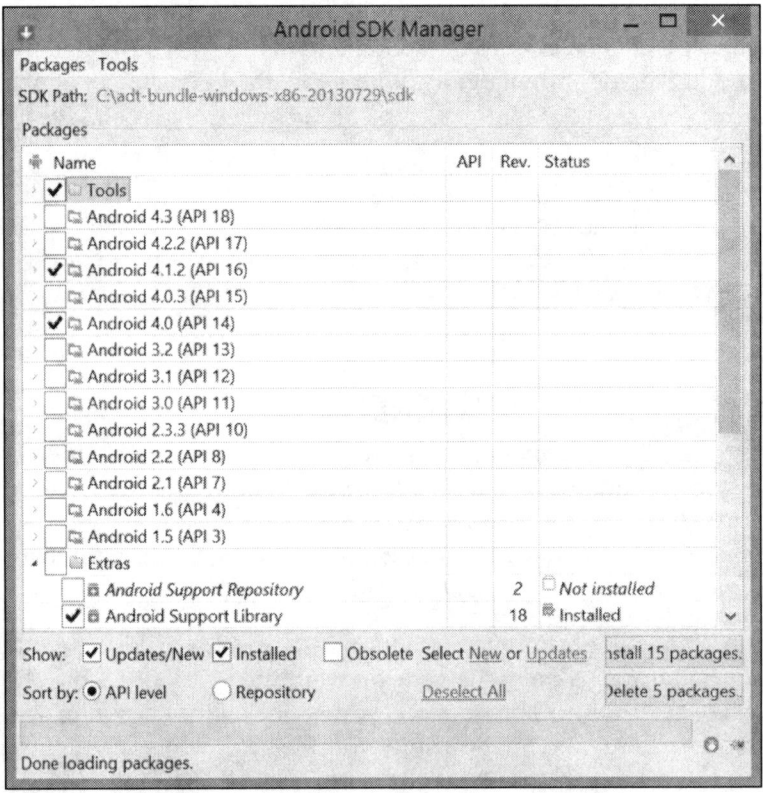

Ouya requires certain Android APIs to be installed that are not pre-installed by default. To install the others you'll need to check:

- **Tools**
- **Android 4.1.2 (API 16)**
- **Android 4.0 (API 14)**
- **Extra/Android Support Library**

Click on **Install Packages** and you will be presented with a license window. Click on **Accept Licenses**. Now is a good time to get yourself a drink as the install can take quite a while.

> Google has changed the path of where some of their tools are installed to. So Ouya finds what it expects we need to copy & paste aapt.exe from (your root Android SDK install folder)/build-tools/17.0.0 to (your root Android SDK install folder)/platform-tools. We copy and paste as the Android SDK expects the aapt.exe to be in the original location.

Setting up the Android NDK

No, that's not a typo! Once we have set up the Android SDK we need to install the Android NDK (Native Development Kit). The NDK is a toolset that allows you to implement parts of your app using native-code languages such as C and C++. The ODK will interface with the NDK and will give you optimum performance in your game.

Perform the following steps to set up the Android NDK:

1. Go to http://developer.android.com/tools/sdk/ndk/index.html in your browser.
2. Select the correct download for your computer, we're going to go with the 32-bit Windows version for this book, and agree to the licensing terms and conditions.
3. Once the file is downloaded, unzip it to the same root folder where you installed the Android SDK.

Connecting Ouya to your Windows computer

The process here is different for Windows 7, Windows 8, and OS X. Let's cover Windows first.

 Windows 8 users will need to disable driver signature verification to install the unsigned Android driver. This involves restarting your PC, so do this before you start. See https://devs.ouya.tv/developers/docs/windows8.md for step-by-step instructions.

Before we get up and running, we need to make sure that Ouya will be recognized by Windows so that we will be able to build to it. The first step of this is to add some paths to your PATH environment variable. This will enable us to run the executables in the Android SDK folder from directory via the command line.

1. Open **My Computer**.
2. From the left-hand panel, right-click on **My Computer** and click on **Properties**.
3. From the left-hand panel, click on **Advanced system settings**.
4. Click on the **Environment Variables…** button.
5. If the PATH variable already exists in the **User variables** table select it and click on the **Edit…** button, else click on the **New…** button.
6. If the PATH variable already exists then append the following to the **Variable value:** (your root Android SDK install folder)/sdk/tools and (your root Android SDK install folder)/sdk/platform-tools.
7. If the PATH variable doesn't exist, type PATH for the **Variable name** and (your root Android SDK install folder)/sdk/tools and (your root Android SDK install folder)/sdk/platform-tools for the **Variable value**.
8. Click on the **OK** button to save your changes.
9. Click on the **OK** button to exit the **Environment Variables** window.
10. Click on the **OK** button to exit the **System Properties** window.

 You will need to change the paths here to match those of your install.

Now open the file from the path: (your root Android SDK install folder)**/sdk/extras/google/usb_driver/android_winusb.inf** in Notepad and paste the code below in both the sections, that is, `[Google.NTx86]` and `[Google.NTamd64]`:

```
;OUYA Console
%SingleAdbInterface%    = USB_Install, USB\VID_2836&PID_0010
%CompositeAdbInterface% = USB_Install, USB\VID_2836&PID_0010&MI_01
```

Save the changes and close the window. Open the **Run** window by pressing the Windows key and *R* or click on **Run** from the Start menu and type `cmd` then click on **OK**.

Type the following in the command prompt window to refresh our data:

`adb kill-server`

`echo 0x2836 >> "%USERPROFILE%\.android\adb_usb.ini"`

`adb start-server`

> It is important that you now check your `adb_usb.ini`. You can find it in your `c:\Users\YOUR_USER_NAME\.android` folder. Open it in Notepad and ensure that the `0x2836` is at the start of a new line. If the first line started with a # then sometimes it is appended to an existing line rather than starting a new one.

Close the window and plug in Ouya to your computer and it should now be recognized. Perform the following steps to install the driver for it:

1. Open the **Device Manager** by right-clicking on **My Computer**.
2. Click on **Properties** and then **Device Manager**.
3. In **Device Manager**, open **Portable Devices** and you should see **OUYA Console**.
4. Right-click on and select **Update Driver Software...**.
5. Click on **Browse my computer for driver software**.
6. Click on **Let me pick from a list of device drivers on my computer**.
7. If you're using Windows 8 then click on **All devices** and then click on **Next**. If you're using Windows 7 this step is not necessary.
8. Click on **Have Disk** and browse to `c:\adt-bundle-windows-x86-\20130729\sdk\extras\google\usb_driver`.
9. Choose **ADB Composite Device**.
10. Accept the unsigned driver.

Setting Up Unity and the Ouya Plugin

Turn on Ouya and wait for the menu screen to appear on your TV. Make sure no other Android devices are attached to your computer. Now, open the command prompt and type `adb devices`. If all has gone according to plan, you should see a device listed as the following screenshot:

```
C:\Users\Gary Riches>adb devices
* daemon not running. starting it now on port 5037 *
* daemon started successfully *
List of devices attached
015d3f18ac0bf418        device
```

If not, go back and check again whether you've completed the all the preceding steps. Common fail points are your `adb_usb.ini` having `0x2836` appended to an existing line rather than being on a new one or the number being typed incorrectly. Also try killing and starting the ADB server again with the `adb kill-server` and `adb start-server` commands we used earlier.

Connecting Ouya to your Mac computer

While the process for installing the required software is similar, the process for getting Ouya recognized by the OS is different.

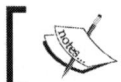 You will need to change the paths here to match to your installation process.

We're going to have to add some paths to PATH. Assuming that you have put the SDK folder in the location `~/Development/adt-bundle-mac-x86_64`, open up a **Terminal** window (this is in your `Applications/Utilites` folder by default). Enter the following command:

`open ~/.bash_profile`

This will open the `.bash_profile` file in **TextEdit** (the default text editor included on your Mac). This file allows you to customize the environment your user runs in. Add the following three lines:

```
export PATH=$PATH:~/Development/adt-bundle-mac-x86_64/sdk/tools
export PATH=$PATH:~/Development/adt-bundle-mac-x86_64/sdk/platform-tools
export ANDROID_HOME=~/Development/adt-bundle-mac-x86_64/sdk
```

Save the file and quit TextEdit. Now we've made the changes that are needed to execute the file. Type the following in **Terminal**:

`source ~/.bash_profile`

Now add the following line to `~/.android/adb_usb.ini` (create it if it doesn't exist) for your `OUYA Console` to be recognized:

    0x2836

>  There should be no carriage return after the hex value. Any blank lines in this file will result in an error.

Make sure your Ouya is connected and turned on and in **Terminal**, type the following:

    adb kill-server
    adb start-server
    adb devices

If you see a device listed in your **Terminal** window then all is well, if not, check that you have installed all the required software, your device is turned on, and that you have connected it via USB.

Ouya Development Kit

We're almost ready to get in to Unity but we still have to install the ODK first. Go to `https://devs.ouya.tv/developers/odk` in your browser. Press the red button that says **Download ODK**. Once the file is downloaded, unzip it to the same root folder where you installed the Android SDK.

Go to `https://github.com/ouya/ouya-unity-plugin` in your browser. The **Ouya Unity** files are stored in **GitHub**. If you're comfortable using GitHub you should clone the repository, if you're not comfortable with it then you should use the **Download ZIP** button on the right-hand side of the page.

Once the file is downloaded, unzip it to the same root folder where you installed the Android SDK.

> Understanding how to use GitHub is a useful skill that will help you in many projects, not just this one. Have a read of the **GitHub Help** page located at `https://help.github.com/`

[21]

The Unity project

Instead of giving us developers a `unitypackage` file to download, the Ouya team give us a Unity project and we need to build it ourselves. The benefit of this is that the Ouya team can update the files on GitHub and, if we have cloned the repository, we'll be able to pull an update easily and rebuild the packages. The following steps will guide you through creating the Ouya `unitypackage` file that, after importing, will enable us to configure the Ouya project settings and allow us to deploy to Ouya itself:

1. Open Unity and navigate to **File** | **Open Project** | **Open Other**. You'll need to navigate to where you unzipped the Ouya Unity files and press **Select Folder**. Depending on how up-to-date the files are you may get a message from Unity about upgrading the project, if it asks for an upgrade, then let it proceed.

2. To generate the `unitypackage` file, we will need to configure the Ouya project settings which on importing will allow us to deploy to Ouya itself. Click on **OUYA** | **Export Core Package** and after a short delay a window will open and you should see a file named `OuyaSDK-Core`.

3. We're now going to create a new Unity project. We'll need to set it to be for the Android platform, set up the Android requirements, and then set up the Ouya-specific requirements. Create a new project in Unity, call it `Sokoban`, and navigate to **File** | **Build Settings**, then click on **Android** and click on **Switch Platform**. Now click on the **Player Settings** button from the same window. A tab should appear, click on **Other Settings** and then click on the drop-down box next to **Minimum API Level**, you will need to select **Android 4.1 'Jelly Bean' (API Level 16)**. Next, click on **Resolution and Presentation** and set the **Default Orientation** to **Landscape Left**.

4. Finally, navigate to **Assets** | **Import Package** | **Custom Package...** and select the `OuyaSDK-Core` file that was created a moment ago. Import all the files and then, once they have processed, you will see a new menu item at the top of the screen: **OUYA**.

The bundle identifier

Each game for Ouya must have a unique bundle identifier. A bundle identifier is used to identify your app in the app store, link purchases from the app to your account, and let other processes know what is running.

Because Unity interfaces with Ouya as an Android app with a Java plugin it means there are three bundle identifiers: one for the Unity project, one for the `Android Manifest` file, and one for the Java plugin, if there are any mismatches your app won't deploy on to Ouya. The first step is coming up with your bundle identifier, they are normally created in reverse-domain notation, for example: `com.companyName.productName`. For the purposes of this book we'll use `com.generic.sokoban`.

Thankfully, Ouya now provides a way to sync the bundle identifier from Unity in to the two other places.

In the Player Settings menu, click on the Android icon and then click on **Other Settings** and then type the bundle identifier in the textbox marked **Bundle Identifier***.

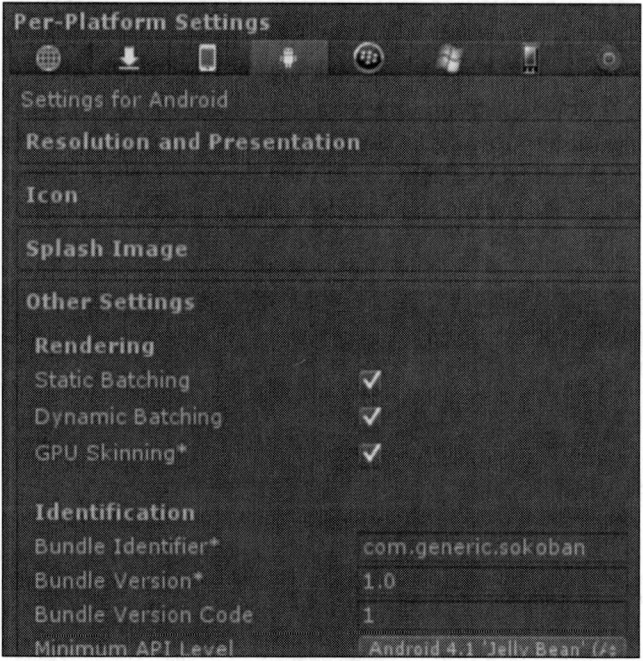

Navigate to **Window | Open Ouya Panel**. A panel will appear and you will most likely see a **[error] (bundle mismatched)** warning. Click on **Sync Bundle ID** and after a few moment that warning should go away.

Setting up Ouya Panel

The following is the screenshot of **Ouya Panel**, you use it to configure all the paths that the Ouya Unity plugin requires.

Click on the third tab, **Java JDK**, and then click on **Download JDK 6 32-bit**. A browser will open and you will need to accept the license agreement and then click on **Windows x86**. Oracle will ask you to sign in, do so if you already have an account, if not then create one and download the Java JDK. Run the installer and leave all the options as default, once it's finished head back over to Unity. Click on **Select SDK Path...** and then navigate to the default install location of the **Java JDK**, for me the location is c:/Program Files (x86)/Java/jdk1.6.0_45.

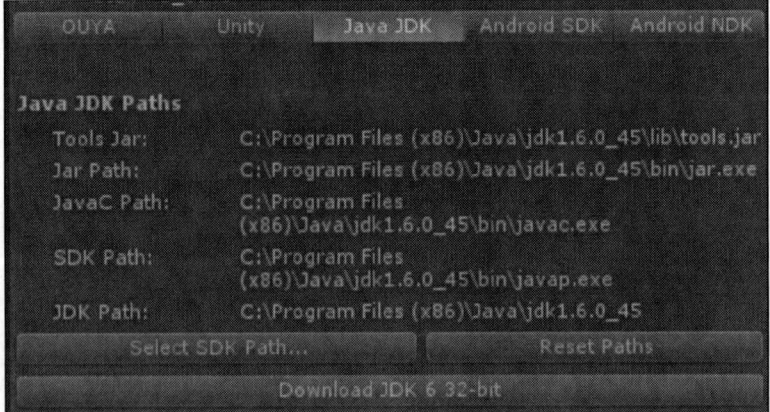

Now click on the fourth tab, **Android SDK**, and then click on **Select SDK Path...** and navigate to your root Android SDK folder.

For me the location is `c:/adt-bundle-windows-x86-20130729/sdk`. The labels at the top of the panel should go from gray to white. If the **APT Path** is still gray then make sure you copied the `aapt.exe` from (your root Android SDK install folder)/`build-tools/17.0.0` to (your root Android SDK install folder)/`platform-tools`.

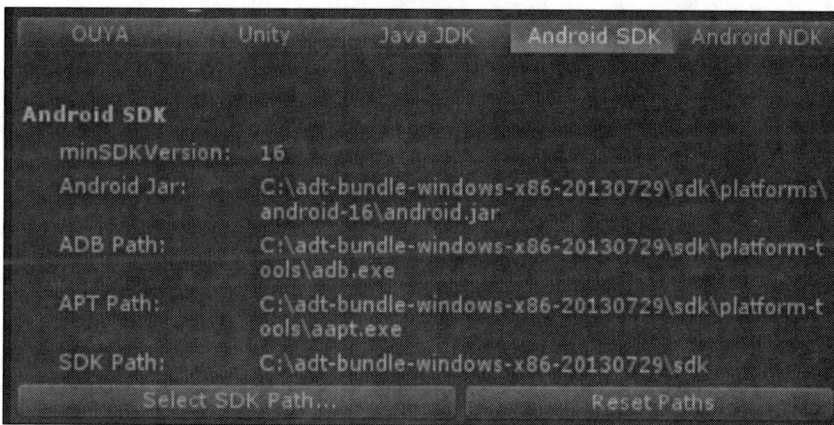

Finally, we have to set up the **Android NDK** paths. Click on the fifth tab, **Android NDK**, and then click on **Select NDK Path...** and navigate to your root Android NDK folder. Now click on **Select NDK Make Path...** and navigate to your (root Android NDK folder)/`prebuilt/windows/bin/make.exe`.

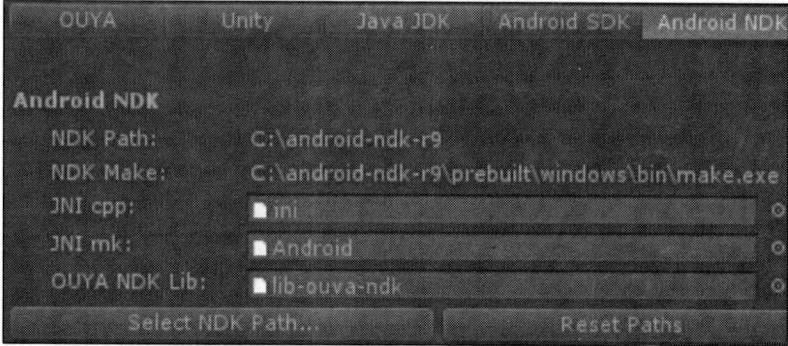

Now the Java JDK, Android SDK, and Android NKD have been set up, we need to compile everything. The **Ouya Panel** makes this really easy. Click on the first tab, **OUYA**, and you will see three buttons:

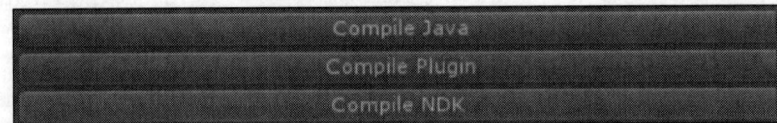

Press each one in turn, you should see results in the console, hopefully with no errors. If you do have errors, read them carefully as they usually explain what the issue is. It's normally to do with one of the tabs being set up incorrectly so check each tab in turn, ensuring all the fields that have path names are in white, not gray.

That's **Ouya Panel**, set up and configured properly. While it does seem like a long process to set it up, it saves your configuration so you only need to do it the once.

Ouya required prefabs

Open the **Project** panel in Unity and navigate to **Ouya | SDK | Editor | Prefabs | OuyaGameObject**. Drag an instance of this prefab in to the scene and select it. In the **Inspector** panel you will see a **DEVELOPER_ID** field, you will need to paste your Developer ID in there. If you don't know what yours is then log in at `https://devs.ouya.tv/developers`. You'll see *Developer UUID (used for configuring in-app purchases)*. Copy the Developer ID from there and paste it in to the **DEVELOPER_ID** field in Unity.

Building, running, and compiling an application

We're now ready to see all your hard work so far pay off.

If you have the basic version of Unity then click on **Compile** on the **Ouya Panel** and you'll see few command prompts open and close, when it's finished navigate to **File | Build & Run**.

If you have the pro version of Unity then you can use the **Build, Run and Compile Application** button. Click on it and you'll see a few command prompts open and then close, followed by the Unity build progress bar.

 For the purposes of this book, if you see **Build, Run and Compile Application** use the correct method for your version of Unity.

If all has gone according to plan, in a few moments you'll see a Unity splash screen followed by the blue hue of your default scene and main camera.

Common fail points here are Unity not finding the Ouya or the app opening and then closing immediately. If Unity cannot find the Ouya make sure you have followed all the steps from the *Connecting Ouya to your Windows/Mac computer* section of this chapter. If the app is opening and then immediately closing again, make sure you have added the required prefabs and entered your Developer ID in to the **OuyaGameObject** prefab. If it is still opening and then immediately closing, make sure you have also compiled the Java JDK, the Android SDK, and the Android NDK, as described in the *Setting up Ouya Panel* section of this chapter.

You can breathe a sigh of relief now, that's the boring bit over with.

Summary

If you've made it this far then well done! The process of setting up Unity for Ouya development is not a simple one and there are many steps which can fail. Now the required software is installed, setting up Ouya Panel again is a lot less painful. In the next chapter, we'll be getting to the fun stuff. Let's go!

3
Setting Up Your Game

After the history lesson and setting up your project you must be looking forward to do some actual development. In this chapter, we'll be explaining the difference between three of the languages you can use to program in Unity, creating a basic structure for our game, creating a title screen, creating an in-game screen, and rendering a level.

Boo, C#, or UnityScript

Unity is amazing. With minimal effort you can have a prototype up and running in a few hours. No other engine has allowed such great flexibility. Another of Unity's excellent features is the ability to program in three languages, namely **C#**, **UnityScript**, and **Boo**. Let's go in to the pros and cons of each one, and explain which one we'll be using.

Boo

Boo is an object-oriented, statically-typed programming language that has a syntax inspired by **Python**. Boo has only been covered here for completeness, the documentation for programming in Unity with Boo is poor to non-existent and only around 5 percent of Unity developers actually use Boo, so finding support when you need it could prove difficult.

UnityScript

If you know JavaScript then you'll feel comfortable with UnityScript. The syntax is exactly the same; you just need to learn all the addressable objects from Unity. Both JavaScript and UnityScript support **dynamic typing**. This is great if you are just trying to create something quickly and don't want to worry too much with the details, but it can lead to less manageable code and dynamic typing is not supported on iOS. Some plugins, which you can buy on the asset store, will be written in UnityScript, but these will often require modification to get them running on all platforms.

C#

C# is also an object-oriented language, like Boo, but the similarities end there. C# is a multiparadigm programming language; a framework where programmers are free to work in a variety of styles, mixing **constructs** from different paradigms. It encompasses strong typing, declarative, imperative, procedural, functional, object-oriented and component-oriented programming disciplines. The majority of plugins you can buy on the asset store are written in C# and will work on mobile with very little code changes, if any. Unity requires that all variables are strongly typed, which means that any issues with the code will be identified within Unity and will stop you compiling until they are resolved. This makes it a lot less error prone than Boo or UnityScript, and it is for this reason that we will be writing our game, **Sokoban**, in C#.

The project structure

Keeping your Unity project in a good shape is important. Things can quickly get out of hand as a project goes from small prototype to full on work-in-progress. Normally, you have good intentions to tidy it up at a later date but the deadlines and bugs always seem to get in the way. Setting up the project structure before you start, and sticking to it as you go along, will save you a lot of time as you won't be searching for files later on when you could be programming.

You should still have your Sokoban project from *Chapter 2, Setting Up Unity and the Ouya Plug-in*, so we'll carry on from that point. So far the project is set up so that the platform is Android and we have imported the OuyaSDK-Core unity package. This will have created some folders already in your project. Make the project panel visible by clicking on **Window | Project**; there should already be some folders there, namely LitJson, Ouya, and Plugins. We're going to create some new folders to hold other files in project, so click on the **Create** drop-down menu, which is located just underneath the **Project** tab in panel you opened. A menu should appear which will save your time in the future, so get accustomed to what you can create from here.

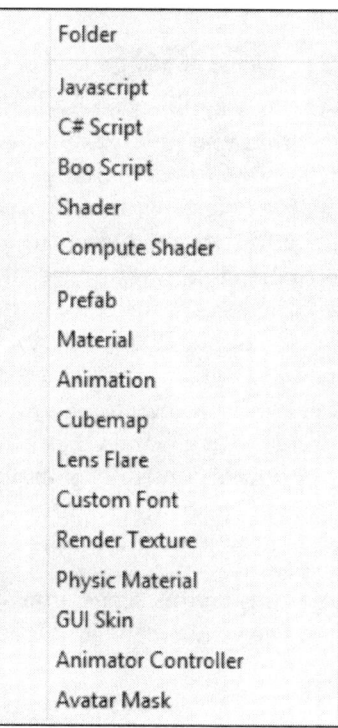

Setting Up Your Game

Click on **Folder** and a new folder will be created in the project panel. Here you can type the name and click on **Return**, and the folder will be created. We need to create folders for the following directories:

- `Materials`
- `Prefabs`
- `Scenes`
- `Scripts`

Setting up your Scenes

You should now have a project panel with seven folders and a scene with **Main Camera** and **OuyaGameObject** that you have entered your developer ID into. We are going to use this scene as a setup scene that isn't displayed for long but instead adds all the required game objects. Normally in Unity, when loading a new scene, all objects are destroyed, and then the objects in the new scene are loaded. If it is needed to have an object persist between scenes then there is a method, `DontDestroyOnLoad` that you can pass an object to. If the object is a component or GameObject then its entire transform hierarchy will not be destroyed either. A side effect of this is that if the scene has the GameObject added to it in Unity and you load it multiple times (on a level select screen for example) then the GameObject will be cloned multiple times and, with a GameObject that handles controller input for example, this can result in multiple controller presses being triggered. We can avoid this by having all our GameObjects that require `DontDestroyOnLoad` being instantiated on a scene that we will only ever load the one time.

As we won't be displaying anything on this scene, you should delete **Main Camera**. We'll also need a mechanism to leave this scene and load the next one, by performing the following steps:

1. Save the current scene as `SetUp` by clicking on **File | Save Scene**, and select the **Scenes** folder you created earlier.

2. While we're dealing with scenes, let's create another one we're going to be using shortly. Click on **File | New Scene**, and select the **Scenes** folder you created earlier. Give it a name of `TitleScreen` and click on **Save**.

3. Repeat these steps to create a scene named **GameScreen** too. This will have left us in the wrong scene, so double-click on our **SetUp** scene again to load that one.

4. Your final setup should look like the following screenshot:

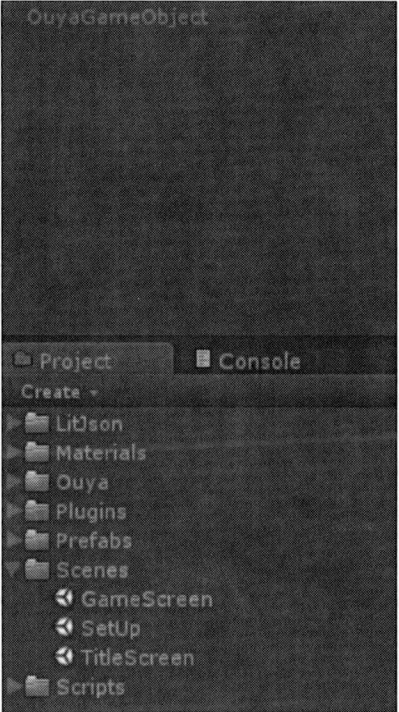

Scripts and MonoDevelop

Click on **GameObject** | **Create Empty** and a new GameObject will appear on the stage with the name **GameObject**. It should already be highlighted, so click it once more and the name will become editable, call it `AdvanceToNextLevel`.

We're going to create and attach a C# sharp script to the `AdvanceToNextLevel` GameObject that will load a new scene as soon as this one is initialized. Right-click on the `Scripts` folder you created earlier and then click on **Create** and select the **C# Script** label. Once you click on it, a script will appear in the `Scripts` folder and it should already have focus and be asking you to type a name for the script, call it `AdvanceToNextLevel`. Double-click on the script in Unity and it will open MonoDevelop, which is an open source, integrated development environment that runs on Linux, Mac OSX, and Windows. It supports automatic code completion, source control, and **Graphical User Interface (GUI)**.

After MonoDevelop has loaded, you will be presented with the C# stub code that was created automatically for you by Unity when you created the C# script.

Let's break down what's currently there before we replace some of it with new code. At the top you will see the following two lines of code:

```
using UnityEngine;
using System.Collections;
```

The `UnityEngine` namespace contains interfaces and class definitions that let MonoDevelop know about all the addressable objects inside Unity.

The `System.Collections` namespace contains interfaces and classes that define various collections of objects, such as **lists**, **queues**, **bit arrays**, **hash tables**, and **dictionaries**. We won't be using the `System.Collections` in this script, so we can go ahead and delete that line although it won't affect if you leave it in.

The next line of code you'll see is as follows:

```
public class AdvanceToNextLevel : MonoBehaviour {
```

The class name must match the filename. When Unity created our C# stub code, it took care of this, we can see this result as our file is named `AdvanceToNextLevel` and the class is also named `AdvanceToNextLevel`. Next up is the `: MonoBehaviour` section of the code. All behavior scripts must inherit from `: MonoBehaviour` directly or indirectly. While this happens automatically in JavaScript, it must be explicitly declared inside the C# scripts. If you create your script inside Unity through the **Create | C# Script**, the created template will already contain the necessary definition.

The line after that is a method definition for a method named `Start`, as shown in the following code. It isn't a user method, but one that belongs to `MonoBehaviour`.

```
void Start () {

}
```

Downloading the example code

You can download the example code files for all Packt books you have purchased from your account at http://www.packtpub.com. If you purchased this book elsewhere, you can visit http://www.packtpub.com/support and register to have the files e-mailed directly to you.

`Start` is called just before any of the `Update` methods are called for the first time. We're not going to use `Start`; we're going to use `Awake` instead, so you can change the word `Start` to `Awake` as the method signatures are the same. This is the method that will load our next scene.

`Start` is only called once in the lifetime of the behavior. The difference between `Awake` and `Start` is that `Start` is only called if the script instance is enabled. This allows you to delay any initialization code until it is really needed. `Awake` is always called before any `Start` method functions. This allows you to order the initialization of your scripts.

Inside the curly braces add the following line to the code:

```
Application.LoadLevel("TitleScreen");
```

`LoadLevel` will simply destroy everything in the current scene, excluding GameObjects that have `DontDestroyOnLoad` set, and load the scene specified as a string. The string is the filename of the scene, in this case `TitleScreen`, which we created earlier.

The last piece of code is the `Update` method. This method is called once every frame so it's an ideal place to add any code that will need to execute constantly such as checks for movement. This particular script has no need for the method, so go ahead and delete it.

Your final script should look like the following code:

```
usingUnityEngine;

public class AdvanceToNextLevel : MonoBehaviour {

  // Use this for initialization
  void Awake () {
    Application.LoadLevel("TitleScreen");
  }
}
```

Now we have finished our first script, we need to attach it to a GameObject in our scene. Go back to Unity and you'll see a small activity indicator in the lower-right of the screen, that's your script being compiled and checked for errors by Unity. If there are ever any issues, they will appear in the console. Drag your `AdvanceToNextLevel` script to your `AdvanceToNextLevel` GameObject.

Scene progression

We have to add the scenes that we're going to use to the build settings before we can test our code works, so click on **File | Build Settings**, and then click on **Add Current**. You'll see the scene name appear in the **Scenes In Build** area, now drag the **TitleScreen** and the **GameScreen** scenes into the same window and their names will appear there too. Close the build settings window and click on the play icon in the top-middle of the Unity screen. If all has worked as expected you should be staring back at a plain blue screen. That's actually a good result as it means your **SetUp** scene is working as expected and has loaded the **TitleScreen** scene immediately, and the blue screen you see is from the background color of **Main Camera** in that scene.

> Make sure you click on the play icon again to stop the play mode, this is important as any changes you make in play mode are not permanent and will reset to the default values when play mode is disabled.

The title screen menu

Double-click on the **TitleScreen** scene in the `Scenes` folder to load that scene. We're going to need some kind of instructions on the **TitleScreen** scene, let's keep it simple for now. Click on **GameObject | Create Other | 3D Text**. A new **Text Mesh** component will appear in the **Hierarchy** panel with the name **New Text** and **Inspector** panel will show **Text Mesh**. **New Text** should already be highlighted, so click it once more to rename it and call it `Play Instructions`, then click on **Return**. Now drag it in to the **Main Camera** to make it a child object of the **Main Camera**. Click on the **Main Camera** and in the **Inspector** panel, and you should see **Background** with a blue hue next to it, click on the blue color and a palette will appear in a new window. Move the blue hue to the black hue, and then close the window.

Select the text in the **Inspector** panel and replace the text that's there, **Hello World** with the text `Press O to Play`. Change the anchor from upper-left to middle-center and change the font size to `50`. The text has been set and added to the correct GameObject but we need to position it correctly, in the **Inspector** panel set the position to `X: 0, Y: 0, Z: 50`, and then click on the play icon to test the scene. You should see something like the following screenshot:

Advancing to the game

We'll add keyboard support first, and then once we know all our scripts are working, we'll add Ouya controller support.

> It's important to implement one feature at a time because if something goes wrong, it can make debugging much harder if there are multiple failure points.

Right-click on the `Scripts` folder in your **Project** panel and navigate to **Create | C# Script**. Call the new script as `ControlsTitleScreen`, and then double-click on the script to edit it in MonoDevelop. You'll see that the `Start` and `Update` methods have already been created. In the `Update` method, we're going to check if the *Space* key has been pressed to start the game. We'll break it down after, but the code we need to add now is as follows:

```
void Update () {
  if(Input.GetKeyDown(KeyCode.Space)){
    Application.LoadLevel("GameScreen");
  }
}
```

The preceding code is going to check every frame, if the key with the `KeyCode` of `Space` has been pressed that frame. We are just using `Space` when testing in the editor; we'll be adding Ouya controller support in the next section. You can also use `GetKey()` to detect the key being held over multiple frames. We used `LoadLevel` earlier so that we should understand what that does but just to refresh your memory, it will simply destroy everything in the current scene, excluding GameObjects that have `DontDestroyOnLoad` set, and load the scene specified as a string. The string is the filename of the scene, in this case **GameScreen**, which we created earlier. Save your script and go back to Unity, we're done for now.

Click on **GameObject** | **Create Empty**, and a new GameObject will appear in the **Hierarchy** panel with the name **GameObject**. It should already be highlighted, so click on it once more and the name will become editable, call it `Controls`. Drag the `ControlsTitleScreen` script from the **Project** panel to the `Controls` GameObject.

Click on the play icon to test your scene. It should start off with a black screen with the text **Press O to Play** on it, and then go to the blue screen when the *Space* key is pressed.

Ouya controller support

Assuming that everything now works as it should, let's get the title screen detecting Ouya input and then giving it a run on the Ouya itself to check everything is working as expected. The Ouya code examples are updated frequently, so are often hosted on GitHub for version control and ease of access. The code for accessing input is no different and can be found at `https://github.com/rendermat/OuyaInputFramework`. As before, if you are familiar with GitHub then you will be better in off cloning the repository, else click on the **Download ZIP** button located on the right-hand side of the page. For the time being we're only interested in one file from the ZIP, namely `OuyaInput.unitypackage`.

1. Double-click on **OuyaInput.unitypackage** and it will open in Unity and ask you what you want to import.
2. Uncheck **Documentation**, **Prefabs**, and **Scenes**, and then click on **Import**. If you want to learn more you can import everything and load up the scene named `ControllerSimpleTest`. There you can see all input being handled from the Ouya controller.
3. After the import has finished, you will see a C# script named **OuyaInput** in the `Plugins` folder. The code inside this script is defined as a static class, which means we do not have to attach it to a GameObject for it to work.

4. Double-click on your **ControlsTitleScreen** script in the **Project** panel to edit it in MonoDevelop and add the following code just above the Start method:

   ```
   public bool continuousScan = true;
   public OuyaPlayer player = OuyaPlayer.P01;
   ```

   The first variable, continuousScan, is going to be used a little further down, so we'll deal with that when we come to it.

   The second variable, player, is being set to an integer value with a predefined name, this is called enum. This will be passed to the GetButtonDown method, so it knows what controller to read the values from.

5. Add the following lines inside the Start method:

   ```
   OuyaInput.SetContinuousScanning(continuousScan);
   OuyaInput.UpdateControllers();
   ```

   Passing true to SetContinuousScanning will allow us to receive button up and down events from the controller. UpdateControllers will grab the initial state from the controllers.

6. At the top of the Update method, add the following code:

   ```
   OuyaInput.UpdateControllers();
   ```

7. Update the if statement we used to check for the *Space* key being pressed. Change that line to the following:

   ```
   if (Input.GetKeyDown(KeyCode.Space) || OuyaInput.GetButtonDown(OuyaButton.O, player)){
   ```

   You can see we have added the OR operator, ||, if you read the code now, it should all seem quite clear: if the *Space* key or the *O* key is down for player 1, then use the following code.

   The final script should look like the following code:

   ```
   using UnityEngine;
   using System.Collections;

   public class ControlsTitleScreen : MonoBehaviour {

       // Do we want to scan for trigger and d-pad button events?
       publicboolcontinuousScan = true;

       // The player we want to get input for
   ```

Setting Up Your Game

```
    publicOuyaPlayer player = OuyaPlayer.P01;

    // Use this for initialization
    void Start () {

        // Set button state scanning to receive input state
        events for trigger and d-pads
        OuyaInput.SetContinuousScanning(continuousScan);

        // Do a controller update here to get everything
        started as soon as possible
        OuyaInput.UpdateControllers();
    }

    // Update is called once per frame
    void Update () {

        // Update the controllers here for best results
        OuyaInput.UpdateControllers();

        if (Input.GetKeyDown(KeyCode.Space) ||
          OuyaInput.GetButtonDown(OuyaButton.O, player)){
          Application.LoadLevel("GameScreen");
        }
      }
    }
}
```

That's it for the Ouya controller support for the `TitleScreen` at the moment. Make sure your Ouya is turned on and connected to your computer, and click on **Build**, **Run**, and **Compile Application** on the Ouya Panel. Your game should start and present a black screen with **Press O to Play** on it, press *O* on your controller and the screen should change from black to blue. Let's stop that screen being so bare.

Creating the level

Start by opening the **GameScreen** scene you created earlier by double-clicking on it. There should just be a **Main Camera** and nothing else. Make the background color of the **Main Camera** black, just like you did earlier, and set the position to X: 3, Y: 6, Z: -10.

Prefabs

A **prefab** is a type of asset, a reusable GameObject that is accessible from the **Project** panel. Prefabs can be added into any scene, multiple times per scene. When you add a prefab to a scene, an instance is created of it. All prefab instances are linked to the original prefab. No matter how many instances exist in your project, when you make a change to the prefab, you will see the change applied to all instances of it.

Creating a Prefab

In order to create a prefab, drag a GameObject that you've created in the scene into the **Project** panel, we're using the Prefabs folder to store ours. The GameObject's name will turn blue to show that it is a prefab.

We're going to need five prefabs in our game; a wall, a floor, a goal, a crate, and a player. Let's just use cubes for now, we can pretty things up later. Click on **GameObject | CreateOther | Cube**, and a cube will appear in your **Hierarchy** panel. Click on it to select it, then click on **Edit | Duplicate**, you'll need to keep doing that until you have created five cubes in total. Click on each one in turn and rename it. Call them wall, floor, goal, crate, and player. Before we make them prefabs, we need to set up the transform of some of them.

Click on the goal GameObject and in the **Information** panel, set the scale to X: 1, Y: 0.1, Z: 1, and then do the same with the floor GameObject.

Drag each of the new GameObjects in to the Prefabs folder we created in the **Projects** panel. They should appear in the folder along with a blue cube icon. The GameObject will remain in the **Hierarchy** panel but the color of its name will have changed from white to blue. Once you have dragged all five GameObjects in the Prefabs folder, you can delete them from the **Hierarchy** panel.

Setting Up Your Game

Materials

Our game would be pretty boring with gray cubes for every single model so let's give them some color. For the purposes of this book, we're just going to use self-illuminating, diffused materials on the prefabs, but if you are good with a graphics package you can easily drag a texture into these materials to add some polish to your game. Right-click on the `Materials` folder in your **Project** panel and click on **Create** | **Material**. Call the new material wall. In the **Inspector** panel, click on the drop-down menu next to **Shader** and select **Self-Illumin** | **Diffuse**. Just below that, you'll see **Main Color** with a white color swatch next to it. Click on the swatch and change the color to red then close the color palette window. With your new material selected, click on **Edit** | **Duplicate**, you'll need to keep doing that until you have created five materials in total. Click on each one of the duplicated materials and rename it. We already have the **wall** material, so call the duplicated ones `floor`, `goal`, `crate`, and `player`. Set colors in the same way as before for each one in turn. Make `floor` as light gray, `goal` as bright green, `crate` as brown, and `player` as blue.

Click and drag each material to its respective prefab, this will assign the material to the prefab and make out game more colorful.

Multidimensional arrays

An array is a reference to a list of objects that you can iterate through numerically. We are going to be storing tile IDs in our array. The ID of the tile will tell us if it's a floor, a wall, a crate, a player or a goal. You will see in the following code that a list is supplied that shows what kind of tile each number represents.

You may have heard of **two-dimensional** arrays, these are arrays where each object is an array; they are useful for storing map data of a tile based game in as you have columns and rows. We're going to be using a **three-dimensional** array. The top-level of the array is going to be the number of the level we're on, each element inside that top-level array will represent a row of the game map and each element of the second-level array is going to be a tile ID.

By using an array to store our level data, it means we can easily store our level layouts in a matter of bytes, and by establishing where our play is in the array we get collision detection for very little effort.

[42]

Create a new C# script in the scripts folder and call it Sokoban, then double-click on the script to edit it. Add the following code just above the Start method:

```csharp
// Legend
// 0 = Floor
// 1 = Wall
// 2 = Goal
// 3 = Crate
// 4 = Player
// -1 = Empty tile


// Create the top array, this will store the level arrays
int [] [] [] levels =
{
  // Create the level array, this will store the row array
  new int [] [] {
    // Create all row array, these will store column data
    new int[] {1,1,1,1,1,1,1,1},
    new int[] {1,0,0,1,0,0,0,1},
    new int[] {1,0,3,3,0,3,0,1},
    new int[] {1,0,0,1,0,1,0,1},
    new int[] {1,0,0,1,3,1,0,1},
    new int[] {1,0,0,2,2,2,2,1},
    new int[] {1,0,0,1,0,4,1,1},
    new int[] {1,1,1,1,1,1,1,1}
  }
};
```

We're only going to have one level for the moment. You can visualize the level quite easily when you look at the three-dimensional array like this.

Now add the following code below the closing bracket of our levels array:

```csharp
public Transform wall;
public Transform floor;
public Transform goal;
public Transform crate;
public Transform player;
int playerRow;
int playerCol;
Transform thePlayer;
string movingCrate = "";
int amountOfCrates = 0;
```

Setting Up Your Game

Defining the variables here means we will be able to access them from all methods in this class. The ones that are prefixed with public will be exposed inside the Unity development environment. The `playerRow` and `playerCol` methods are going to be used in our level-rendering code and the `crate` related ones are going to be for moving the crates and checking if we've finished the level or not.

The BuildLevel method

We now have the level map in our three-dimensional array, our prefabs to act as the building blocks for our level, and the materials to give them some color, which means we're ready to actually build the level now!

Double-click on your `Sokoban` script to open it in MonoDevelop, and above the `Start` method, add the following code:

```
void BuildLevel () {
  // Loop through the level array
  for (int i = 0; i< levels[0].Length; i++) {

    // Loop through the row array
    for (int j = 0; j < levels[0][i].Length; j++) {

      // What value is the tile in this column
      switch (levels[0][i][j]) {
        case 0: // Floor
        Instantiate(floor,
          new Vector3 (i, -0.6f, j),
        Quaternion.identity);
        break;
        case 1: // Wall, add a floor below it
        Instantiate(
          floor,
          new Vector3 (i, -0.6f, j),
        Quaternion.identity);


        Instantiate(
          wall,
          new Vector3 (i, 0, j),
        Quaternion.identity);
        break;
        case 2: // Goal
```

```
        Instantiate(
          goal,
          new Vector3 (i, -0.6f, j),
        Quaternion.identity);
        break;
        case 3: // Create, add a floor below it
        Instantiate(
          floor,
          new Vector3 (i, -0.6f, j),
        Quaternion.identity);
        Transform crateCubeInstance = Instantiate(
          crate,
          new Vector3 (i, 0, j),
        Quaternion.identity) as Transform;
        crateCubeInstance.name =
        "crate_" + i + "_" + j;
        amountOfCrates++;
        break;
        case 4: // Player, add a floor below it
        Instantiate(
          floor,
          new Vector3 (i, -0.6f, j),
        Quaternion.identity);
        thePlayer = Instantiate(
          player,
          new Vector3 (i,0, j),
        Quaternion.identity) as Transform;
        thePlayer.name = "Player";
        playerRow = i;
        playerCol = j;
        break;
      }
    }
  }
}
```

Setting Up Your Game

That does look like quite a lot of code but it's only using three principles, let's go through what they are:

- The `for` loop: The first `for` loop is iterating through the rows in level 1, we only have one of those so far, so we're just using index 0 in the array. The second for loop is iterating through each column segment in that row.
- The `switch` statement: We pass the tile ID, which we get from the column array, into the switch statement which will evaluate what was passed in and respond with the appropriate case.
- The `Instantiate` method: This is the method that loads the prefabs we created earlier and attaches them to the scene. You will see that we pass `Instantiate` to one of the `public Transform` variables we created earlier.

We have to call the method after creating it so change `Start` to `Awake` and add the method call inside there. The final method should look like the following code:

```
void Awake () {
   BuildLevel();
}
```

As our prefabs are all one unit in size in both X and Z axis, we can just use the `int` that are defined in the `for` loops. As we are setting the walls, player, and crate Y to 0, their Y boundaries will be from -0.5 to 0.5 as Unity will place the center of the GameObject at the location specified. It is for this reason that we set the Y position of the `floor` and `goal` GameObjects to -0.6.

1. Click on **GameObject | Create Empty** and a new GameObject will appear in the **Hierarchy** panel with the name **GameObject**.
2. It should already be highlighted, so click on it once more and the name will become editable; call it `Sokoban`.
3. Drag the `Sokoban` script to the GameObject, and you will see your five exposed, public `Transform` variables in the **Inspector** panel.
4. Click and drag each prefab to its respective **Transform** variable, this will assign the prefab to the variable.

5. Click on **Build, Run and Compile Application** on the **Ouya** panel, and then proceed past the title screen and you should hopefully see a screen like the following screenshot:

Common fail points are forgetting to add the script to a new GameObject in this scene or neglecting to add the prefabs to the exposed public `Transform` variables in the **Inspector** panel.

Summary

We've laid a lot of groundwork in this chapter, so well done. You should now understand the different coding options available to you and their pros and cons and your Unity project should also be set up in a way that will help you work smarter in the future. We also achieved our first Ouya specific programming with the controller input. In *Chapter 4, Adding a Character and Making Them Move*, we'll give you a better camera angle, make your character move and add some animation.

4
Adding a Character and Making Them Move

From the previous chapter, you should have a very colorful view when you test the game, but it's somewhat lacking in interactivity. We're going to add movement to our basic character and get the **Main Camera** game object in Unity following them around the level as they move. We'll also add in the ability for them to push crates around the level. Finally, we'll swap out our existing character for something that is a bit fancier and trigger their built in animations as they move around the level.

Making the camera move

The first thing you hopefully noticed when we tested the scene in the previous chapter was that we were just looking in to the distance at nothing. That won't do for a game, traditionally the camera follows the player around the level and responds to their movements. The character in our game at the moment is represented by a blue cube, in our `BuildLevel` method of our `Sokoban` script, we assign a name to the player when we instantiate it; to refresh your memory the code in question is as follows:

```
thePlayer = Instantiate(player,
                        new Vector3 (i,0, j),
                        Quaternion.identity) as Transform;
thePlayer.name = "Player";
```

Giving the instantiated `GameObject` a name of `Player` means we will be able to address the `Player` game object from other scripts when we need to reference it.

Adding a Character and Making Them Move

Let's create a new script for making the Main Camera focus on the player and rotate according to the player's orientation. Right-click on the `Scripts` folder that you created earlier and then click on **Create** and select **C# Script**. Once you click on it, a script will appear in the `Scripts` folder, it should already be selected and asking you to type a name for the script, call it `UpdateCameraPosition`. Double-click on the script in Unity and it will open **MonoDevelop**. The aim of this script will be to:

- Find the player
- Move the Main Camera game object to a fixed distance from them
- Rotate to position the Main Camera game object behind the player

Unity provides a method to find any `GameObject`, conveniently called `Find`, although it's a very expensive operation to call. If no game object with that name can be found, `null` is returned. The preferred usage is to find the game object, using `Find`, you want at the initial execution of the script and store a reference to the game object as a variable. Also, you should check that the result is not `null` before you try and use it.

Let's put what we've just learned in to practice and write our Main Camera movement script. As we are going to use `Find` and store the result for reuse later; we will need to create a variable above the `Start` method that has been added automatically for you:

```
Transform target;
```

We will also add a method call to the `Start` and our`Update` method, so add the following line in both methods:

```
PositionCamera();
```

So, we've added the calls to the `PositionCamera` method but we still need to write it. As we have done previously, the code will be written in its entirety; later we can break it down to see what it's doing:

```
void PositionCamera () {

  // If we don't have it then try to find it
  if (target == null) {
    target = GameObject.Find("Player").transform;
  }

  // Is the target still no? If so, then you've named it
  // incorrectly
  if (target == null) {
    return;
```

```
    }

        float angleToReach = Mathf.LerpAngle(transform.eulerAngles.y,
                                             target.eulerAngles.y,
                                             4 * Time.deltaTime);

        Quaternion currentRotation = Quaternion.Euler(0,
                                                      angleToReach,
                                                      0);

        transform.position += target.position + new Vector3(0, 9, 0);
        transform.position -= currentRotation * Vector3.forward * 4;
        transform.LookAt(target.position);
    }
```

As per the Unity documentation, we'll be storing a reference to our `GameObject` rather than calling `GameObject.Find` every frame. If our target variable is not set, we call `target = GameObject.Find("Player").transform`. We only store `transform` as that's all that's needed to adjust the Main Camera's position.

Next up is `angleToReach`, to set this variable we use `Mathf.LerpAngle` which will interpolate the `Vector3` rotation type of the camera's rotation to that of the target's rotation over a period of time. The third argument of `LerpAngle` is the position in `Lerp` (linear interpolation). While you can set an absolute of 0 or 1, for this argument you get a nicer effect by using `Time.deltaTime`. This will normally be quite constant, but as the Main Camera's rotation will be changing each frame, this will give you an easing effect as the Main Camera pans around. We want this to happen quite quickly so we are using `Time.deltaTime` for the position in `Lerp`, hence we are multiplying it by four.

We use the value in `angleToReach` as a variable for the `currentRotation` quaternion and it's going to allow us to work out where the Main Camera game object should be positioned in relation to our target. This is done in a two-step process; first we need to move the Main Camera's position to be over the target and then we need move it along the line of the `angleToReach` float multiplied by `Vector3.forward`. This will give you a position around the target that eases in to place, but by multiplying it by four we can exaggerate the effect.

Finally, now that our Main Camera is orbiting our target and easing in to position, we have to make it actually look at the target. This is very simple in Unity, we just have to call `transform.LookAt(target.position)` and it's as easy as that. This will automatically modify `transform.rotation` of the `Vector3` rotation type to point at the `target.position`.

Close the script, go back to Unity and press the play icon at the top-middle of the Unity screen. If all has gone according to the plan, you should see the Main Camera game object much closer to the player.

Making the character move

Our game is shaping up nicely, we have the level-building code complete and the camera will, in theory, follow the player around when they move. Let's put that to the test.

As in the previous chapter, we'll get all the input working with the keyboard and then implement the Ouya input.

We are going to make it so the person playing the game can turn left, turn right, and move forward. This will always happen one tile at a time.

Edit your `Sokoban` script file and add the following code below the `int amountOfCrates = 0;` line:

```
GameObject theCrate;
bool isPlayerMoving;
bool isPlayerRotating;
int rotationSpeed;
int movingSteps;
int tRow;
int tCol;
```

The items these variables will represent are:

- `theCrate`: This is a reference to the crate game object that the player is currently pushing
- `isPlayerMoving`: This is a Boolean that will be set to `true` if the player is moving, else it will be `false`
- `isPlayerRotating`: This is a Boolean that will be set to `true` if the player is moving, else it will be `false`
- `rotationSpeed`: This indicates how fast the player turn will happen
- `movingSteps`: This indicates the number of steps it will take the movement method to move the player one unit
- `tRow`: This is the row that the player will be attempting to move to
- `tCol`: This is the column that the player will be attempting to move to

The method we're going to add next is going to work out if we can move to the tile when we try to. As we're storing the players X and Y tile position and we know their rotation, we can check the element in the array that represents forwards to the player. The code for this is as follows:

```
// Check if the player is attempting to move
void CheckIfPlayerIsAttempingToMove () {

    // Has the player tried to move forwards?
    if (Input.GetKeyDown (KeyCode.UpArrow)) {

        // What direction is the player currently facing?
        // Depending on the angle we get a different row and
        // column in the array for where we are going to move
        switch((int)Mathf.Round(thePlayer.transform.eulerAngles.y)) {
            case 0 :
            tRow = 0;
            tCol = 1;
            break;
            case 90 :
            tRow = 1;
            tCol = 0;
            break;
            case 180 :
            tRow = 0;
            tCol = -1;
            break;
            case 270 :
            tRow = -1;
            tCol = 0;
```

```
        break;
}

// Is the target tile a floor, 0, or a goal, 2?
if (levels[0][pRow + tRow][pCol+tCol] == 0 ||
    levels[0][pRow + tRow][pCol + tCol] == 2)
{

  isPlayerMoving = true;
  movingSteps = 0;

} else if (levels[0][pRow + tRow][pCol + tCol] == 3 ||
           levels[0][pRow + tRow][pCol + tCol] == 5)
{
  // Is the target tile a crate on a floor tile, 3, or a
  // crate on a goal tile, 5?

  // At this point we know the player is pushing a
  // crate so we need to check if the crate can be
  // pushed to the target location

  // Is the target tile a floor, 0, or a goal, 2?
  if (levels[0][pRow + 2 * tRow][pCol + 2 * tCol] == 0 ||
      levels[0][pRow + 2 * tRow][pCol + 2 * tCol] == 2)
  {

    // Store a reference to the moving crate's name
    movingCrate = "crate_" +
                  (pRow + tRow) +
                  "_" +
                  (pCol + tCol);

    isPlayerMoving = true;
    movingSteps = 0;
  }
 }
} else {

  // Is the player turning left or right?
  // The rotationSpeed variable can be tweaked but MUST go
  // exactly in to 90
  // Example: 90 / 5 = 18 - OK
  // Example: 90 / 6 = 15 - OK
  // Example: 90 / 7 = 12.85 - FAIL
  if (Input.GetKeyDown (KeyCode.RightArrow)) {
    isPlayerRotating = true;
    rotationSpeed = 5;
```

```
      }
      else if (Input.GetKeyDown (KeyCode.LeftArrow)) {
        isPlayerRotating = true;
        rotationSpeed = -5;
      }
    }
  }
}
```

There are comments in the code so you can see, line by line, what each part does, but let's go over the method now, from top to bottom and explain what it does generally:

- Check if the Up arrow key has been pressed. If it has:
    - Check the direction the player is facing and establish what forwards means in terms of which array element to access. Depending on the results of the `switch` statement, it sets `tRow` and `tCol` to the correct values to represent the forwards direction.
    - Check if there is an empty floor or goal tile for the player's target row and column. If there is then we set the `isPlayerMoving` Boolean to `true` and set the `movingSteps` variable to `0`.
    - Check if the tile in front is a crate.
    - If `true` then check if there is an empty floor or goal tile for the crate's target row and column. If there is, then we set the `isPlayerMoving` Boolean to `true`, set the `movingSteps` variable to `0` and store a reference crate's name in `movingCrate`.
- If it hasn't:
    - Check if the Left arrow key has been pressed. If it has, then we set the `isPlayerRotating` Boolean to `true` and set the `rotationSpeed` variable to `-5`.
    - Check if the Right arrow key has been pressed. If it has, then we set the `isPlayerRotating` Boolean to `true` and set the `rotationSpeed` variable to `5`.

Now we have written the method, let's add it in the `Update` method:

```
void Update () {

  // Is the player is stationary at the moment?
  if (!isPlayerMoving && !isPlayerRotating) {
    CheckIfPlayerIsAttempingToMove();
  }
}
```

As you can see, we check if the player is not currently moving or rotating, and if both of those checks pass, we check if the player is attempting to move. While we're working in the `Update` method lets add the next piece of code, add it just below the end of the if statement:

```
if (isPlayerMoving) {
   MovePlayer();
}

// Do we need to rotate the character
// This is an interative process and will occur every frame until
// we have rotated 90 degrees
if (isPlayerRotating) {
   RotatePlayer();
}
```

Let's look at what is happening in the code now:

- `Update` is called once per frame
- If the player is not moving, check if they are attempting to
- If an attempt to move forwards is successful, set `isPlayerMoving` to `true`
- If the player has rotated set `isPlayerRotating` to `true`
- If `isPlayerMoving` is `true`, then call the `MovePlayer` method to move the player model
- If `isPlayerRotating` is `true`, then call the `RotatePlayer` method to rotate the player

Once the `isPlayerMoving` or `isPlayerRotating` Booleans are set to true they will not be set to false until the `MovePlayer` or `RotatePlayer` methods have completed. After we add these next two methods we should be able to test our game and play through the level. Add the following two methods:

```
void MovePlayer () {

   // Move the player forward. We move in 10 steps and need to
   // move 1 unit for 1 complete move
   // so we move 0.1 for each step taken. 0.1 * 10 = 1
   thePlayer.transform.Translate(Vector3.forward * 0.1f);

   // Are we moving a crate?
   if (movingCrate != "") {

      // Get a reference to the crate
      theCrate = GameObject.Find(movingCrate);
```

```
      // What direction is the player currently facing?
      switch((int)Mathf.Round(thePlayer.transform.eulerAngles.y)) {
        case 0 :
        theCrate.transform.Translate(Vector3.forward * 0.1f);
        break;
        case 90 :
        theCrate.transform.Translate(Vector3.right * 0.1f);
        break;
        case 180 :
        theCrate.transform.Translate(Vector3.forward * -0.1f);
        break;
        case 270 :
        theCrate.transform.Translate(Vector3.right * -0.1f);
        break;
      }
    }
  movingSteps++;

  // Have we finished the move?
  if (movingSteps == 10) {

    isPlayerMoving = false;

    // 4 is the tile reference for the player so add 4 to
    // the tile we have moved to
    // Example: A goal, 2, would become 6 as we have added 4
    //for the player
    // Add to the tile we have moved to
    levels[0][pRow + tRow][pCol + tCol] += 4;

    // Remove player from the tile we have moved from
    levels[0][pRow][pCol] -= 4;

    // Are we moving a crate?
    if (movingCrate != "") {

      // 3 is the tile reference for a crate so add 3 to
      //the tile the crate moved to
      // Example: A goal, 2, would become 5 as we have added
      //3 for the crate
      // Add to the tile we have moved to
      levels[0][pRow + 2 * tRow][pCol + 2 * tCol] += 3;

      // Remove from the tile we have moved from
      levels[0][pRow + tRow][pCol + tCol] -= 3;
```

```
            // Adjust the name of the crate and move the
            // reference to it as we are no longer pushing it
            theCrate.name = "crate_" +
                            (pRow + 2 * tRow) +
                            "_" +
                            (pCol + 2 * tCol);
            movingCrate = "";
        }

        // Adjust the stored player location on the map and in
        // the array
        pRow += tRow;
        pCol += tCol;
    }
}

void RotatePlayer () {

    // Adjust the transform
    thePlayer.transform.Rotate(0, rotationSpeed, 0);

    // Have we rotated a full 90 degrees?
    if (Mathf.Round(thePlayer.transform.eulerAngles.y) % 90 == 0)
    {
        isPlayerRotating = false;
    }
}
```

Again, there are comments in the code so that you can see what each part does and gives a general break down of what the code path for each method is. For the `MovePlayer` method:

- Modify player's `transform` by `0.1` of a unit forwards (the direction the player is facing). We use `0.1` as this method will run ten times before setting `isPlayerMoving` to `true`.
- Check if we have a string reference in `movingCrate`.
  - If we do then find the crate
  - Modify crate's `transform` by `0.1` of a unit in the same direction as the player
- Increment the `movingSteps` variable, this is our step counter and we will stop executing this method when this has completed ten steps.
- Check the value of `movingSteps`, if this value is `10` then set the array entries and stop this method being called again.

- Set the value of `isPlayerMoving` to `false`, this is what will stop the method being called in `Update` again until a key press or Ouya controller press occurs.
- Add 4 to the value of the array entry that the player has moved to, this means we can still establish what the original tile is without the player on it.
- Remove four from the array entry we have moved from.
- Check if we have a string reference in `movingCrate`.
  - If we do then add three to the value of the array entry that the crate has moved to
  - Remove three from the array entry the crate has moved from
  - Adjust the crates name to reflect its new position in the array
  - Set `movingCrate` to an empty string in case we don't move it next move
- Modify the `pCol` and `pRow` variables by the values stored in `tCol` and `tRow`, this way we always have the current index of the player.

The `RotatePlayer` method is much simpler:

- Modify player's `transform.Rotate` of the `Vector3` rotation type by the `rotationSpeed` variable defined earlier around the y axis
- Check if we have rotated a full 90 degrees by checking that dividing the current rotation by ninety leaves no remainder. In case you are not sure, the % operator is called modulo
- If we have rotated a full 90 degrees then set `isPlayerRotating` to `false`

Close the script, go back to Unity, and press the play icon at the top middle of the Unity screen. Try using the Left arrow and Right arrow keys to turn left and right and the Up arrow key move forwards. The camera should pan smoothly around the player as you turn.

Ouya controller support

As we have already added the `OuyaInput.unitypackage` package in our previous chapter, we can go right ahead and implement the controller support. The Ouya team have made it so simple to integrate the controller once all the necessary files are imported, just add the following lines inside our public class definition in our `Sokoban` script:

```
public bool continuousScan = true;
public OuyaPlayer player = OuyaPlayer.P01;
```

Also as before, add the following lines to the `Awake` method:

```
OuyaInput.SetContinuousScanning(continuousScan);
OuyaInput.UpdateControllers();
```

At the start of the `Update` method add:

```
OuyaInput.UpdateControllers();
```

Now edit the `CheckIfPlayerIsAttempingToMove` method and edit the following three lines:

```
if (Input.GetKeyDown (KeyCode.UpArrow)) {
if (Input.GetKeyDown (KeyCode.LeftArrow)) {
if (Input.GetKeyDown (KeyCode.RightArrow)) {
```

They need to become:

```
if (Input.GetKeyDown (KeyCode.UpArrow) ||
   OuyaInput.GetButtonDown(OuyaButton.DU, player)) {

if (Input.GetKeyDown (KeyCode.LeftArrow) ||
   OuyaInput.GetButtonDown(OuyaButton.DL, player)) {

if (Input.GetKeyDown (KeyCode.RightArrow) ||
   OuyaInput.GetButtonDown(OuyaButton.DR, player)) {
```

Press **Build, Run and Compile Application** on the **Ouya Panel** and go through the steps to get to the game, try the directional pad on the controller and you'll see that the game responds just as it did when you were pressing the arrow keys on your keyboard.

Animating the character

While there is already some basic animation in the character in terms of moving them smoothly between tiles, wouldn't it be nicer to have an actual character? It would! **Unity Asset Store**, **TurboSquid**, and many others offer models for free or a very low cost. For our game we're going to use an asset that Unity provides in one of their demos. Unity very kindly allows you to include their assets in your own projects and still offer them for sale.

The character in question is from a demo called Astro Dude and he looks like this:

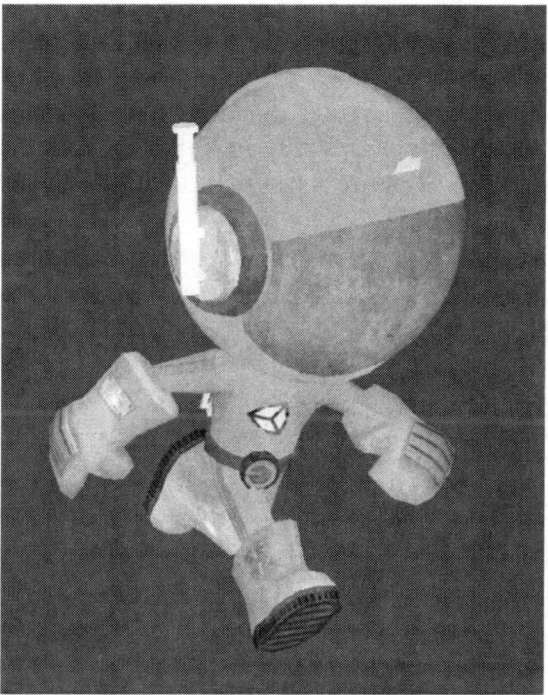

Import the `playerModel.unitypackage` package from the source files for this chapter. Once all the files are imported you'll have a new `Player` folder inside your `Prefabs` folder, click on the **playerAnimated** prefab inside the **PlayerModel** prefab and look at the **Inspector** panel, you should see two animations listed:

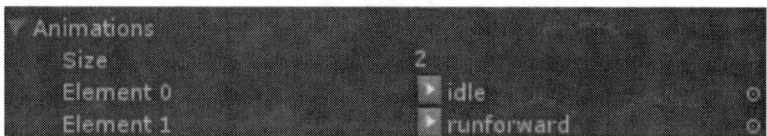

Make a note of the two animation names as we'll be using them later. The names are **idle** and **runforward**.

Drag the new **PlayerModel** prefab in to the `Player` transform slot on the script that is attached to your `Sokoban` game object.

This model's sizes are a little different so we're going to need to adjust the instantiation code in the `BuildLevel` method as we're also going to have to trigger the built in animations already in the model when they are required. Let's start with the model position, it's taller than the one unit that our cube is so to adjust the Y position when we instantiate it change the following line from:

```
thePlayer = Instantiate(player, new Vector3 (i,0, j),
  Quaternion.identity) as Transform;
```

To:

```
thePlayer = Instantiate(player, new Vector3 (i,1, j),
  Quaternion.identity) as Transform;
```

The change is small, we've just changed 0 to 1. There is slightly more code for the animations, but don't worry it's not too much. First we need to declare a variable at the top of our script to store the reference to `Animation` so add the following line inside our public class definition:

```
Animation thePlayerAnimation;
```

If we think about the points we need to trigger our character's animation it's only actually a few places. They are:

- When the script loads, after the `BuildLevel` method, we need to trigger the **idle** animation
- If the Up arrow key is pressed, we need to trigger the **runforward** animation
- If the player has finished moving, we need to trigger the **idle** animation

First we need to get the reference to the animations so add the following lines to the `Awake` method:

```
thePlayerAnimation = GameObject.Find("playerAnimated").animation;
thePlayerAnimation.Play("idle");
```

Next, just after the `GetKeyDown` method check inside the `CheckIfPlayerIsAttemptingToMove` method add:

```
thePlayerAnimation.CrossFade ("runforward");
```

Finally, add to following after the `if (movingSteps == 10) {` line in the `MovePlayer` method:

    thePlayerAnimation.CrossFade ("idle");

Test your game and now and behold! Proper animation and a fancy character in your game.

Summary

What a chapter! We've gone from some colored cubes to something that is actually playable as a game on Ouya. We've now also got camera animation and character animation. As a developer, most of the time you'll work with an artist or buy your assets, so they will come with pre-built animations in them already, the method employed here to animate your character will likely be the most common set of circumstances. Next up we're going to add some finishing touches to our game.

5
Adding Finesse to Your Game

Our game is now playable, and you can progress from the title screen to the game. If you're patient enough, you have even worked out how to finish the level, but don't worry if not, we'll explain the solution shortly. In this chapter, we'll be adding some polish to our game, texturing the cubes, so they fit in more with the design of the main character you added in *Chapter 4*, *Adding a Character and Making Them Move*. We'll also be adding a new level or two, and also indicate when the player has finished the level by playing a fanfare sound.

Texturing your Prefabs

While the mechanics of the game have been developed, we're still using our initial place holder prefabs. We can add a texture to the prefabs really easily and it should hopefully improve the look of the game immensely.

Import the package texturesAndMaterials.unitypackage from the files for this chapter, you should have the following new files:

- `Materials/crate.mat`
- `Materials/moonsurface.mat`
- `Materials/rock_seamless_256.mat`
- `Scripts/AstroDude.shader`
- `Skyboxes/MoonReflection.cubemap`
- `Textures/astrod00d_selfillum.tif`
- `Textures/flag.png`
- `Textures/moonsurface.tif`
- `Textures/moonsurface_normals.tif`
- `Textures/stars.tif`

First things first, we need to update some of the materials and textures to be better suited to our prefabs. Click on **Textures/ rock_seamless_256**, and in the **Inspector** panel, change the **Max Size** to **64** as shown in the following screenshot. Do the same with **rocks_normals, moonsurface**, and **moonsurface_normals**:

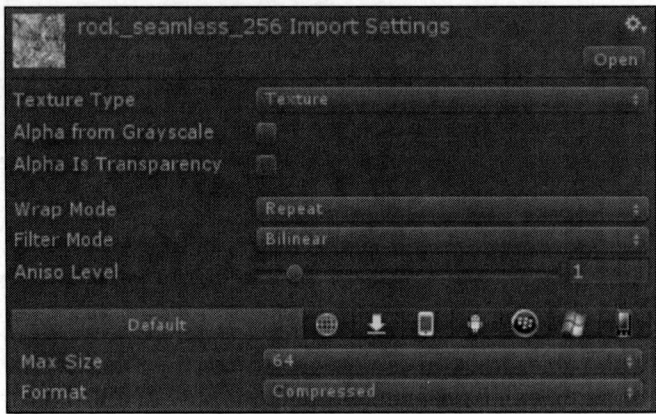

It's because our materials and textures came from the same Astro Dude project that Unity supply that we need to adjust some settings. The next one to change is **Materials/rock_seamless_256** as the old project had the texture being tiled multiple times, we only need it to be tiled the one time. Click on the material in the **Project** panel, and then in the **Inspector** panel, set the tiling for X and Y to 1.

Let's assign our new materials to our prefabs, by performing the following steps. Unity can be quite clever and may have already modified or assigned some of the materials based on their names and the prefabs names.

1. Click and drag the `Crate` material to the `Crate` prefab.
2. Click and drag the `moonsurface` material to the `Floor` prefab.
3. Click and drag the `rock_seamless_256` material to the `Wall` prefab.
4. Click on **Prefabs | Player | Graphics | Materials | astrod00d_diffuse**, and make sure the **Shader** option in the **Inspector** panel is set to **AstroDude**.

The scene is ready to test, but if you did it would be quite dark as we have changed all the materials from self-illuminating to **Diffuse**. To counter this, change the **Ambient Light** panel to 100, 100, 100, and 255. To bring up the **Ambient Light** panel click on **Edit | Render Settings**, and then click on **Ambient Light** in the **Inspector** panel.

Go ahead and click on the play icon at the top-middle of the Unity screen. Marvel at the wonder you have created for a short while, it's getting quite cool, isn't it?

Adding a background

There is still a lot of black in the background and as the game has a space theme, let's add some stars in there. The way we'll do this is to add a sphere that we can map the stars texture to, so click on **Game Object | Create Other | Sphere**, and position it at `X: 0, Y: 0, Z: 0`. We also need to set the size to `X: 100, Y: 100, Z: 100`. Drag the `stars` texture, located at `Textures/stars`, on to the new sphere that we created in our scene. That was simple, wasn't that? Unity has added the texture to a material that appears on the outside of our sphere while we need it to show on the inside. To fix it, we are going to reverse the triangle order, flip the normal map, and flip the UV map with C# code. Right-click on the `Scripts` folder and then click on **Create** and select **C# Script**. Once you click on it, a script will appear in the `Scripts` folder; it should already have focus and be asking you to type a name for the script, call it `SkyDome`. Double-click on the script in Unity and it will open in MonoDevelop. Edit the `Start` method, as shown in the following code:

```
void Start () {

  // Get a reference to the mesh
  MeshFilterBase MeshFilter = transform.GetComponent("MeshFilter")
     as MeshFilter;
  Mesh mesh = BaseMeshFilter.mesh;

  // Reverse triangle winding
  int[] triangles = mesh.triangles;
  int numpolies = triangles.Length / 3;
  for(int t = 0;t <numpolies; t++)
  {
    Int tribuffer = triangles[t * 3];
    triangles[t * 3] = triangles[(t * 3) + 2];
    triangles[(t * 3) + 2] = tribuffer;
  }

  // Read just uv map for inner sphere projection
  Vector2[] uvs = mesh.uv;
  for(int uvnum = 0; uvnum < uvs.Length; uvnum++)
  {
    uvs[uvnum] = new Vector2(1 - uvs[uvnum].x, uvs[uvnum].y);
  }

  // Read just normals for inner sphere projection
  Vector3[] norms = mesh.normals;
  for(int normalsnum = 0; normalsnum < norms.Length; normalsnum++)
  {
```

```
        norms[normalsnum] = -norms[normalsnum];
    }

    // Copy local built in arrays back to the mesh
    mesh.uv = uvs;
    mesh.triangles = triangles;
    mesh.normals = norms;
}
```

The breakdown of the code as is follows:

1. Get the mesh of the sphere.
2. Reverse the way the triangles are drawn. Each triangle has three indexes in the array; this script just swaps the first and last index of each triangle in the array.
3. Adjust the x position for the UV map coordinates.
4. Flip the normals of the sphere.
5. Apply the new values of the reversed triangles, adjusted UV coordinates, and flipped normals to the sphere.

Click and drag this script onto your sphere GameObject and test your scene. You should now see something like the following screenshot:

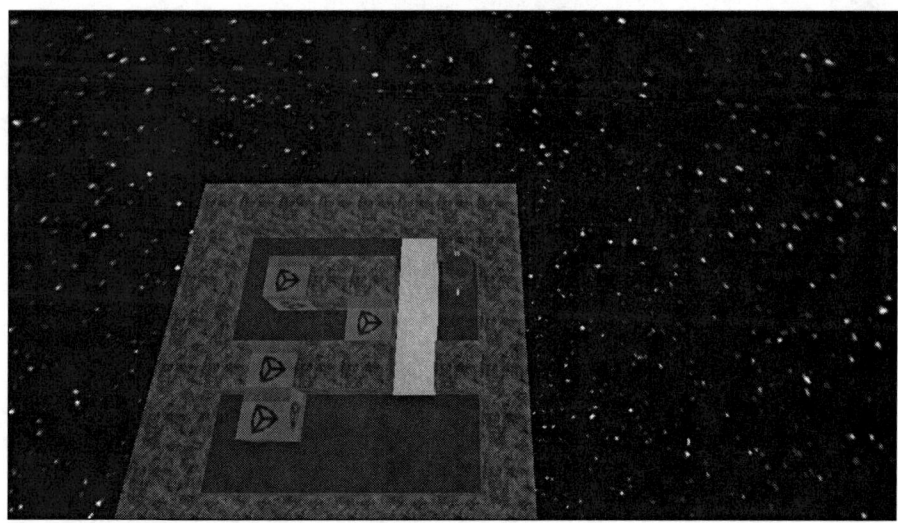

Adding extra levels

Now that the game is looking better, we can add some more content in to it. Luckily the jagged array we created earlier easily supports adding more levels. Levels can be any size, even with variable column heights per row. Double-click on the `Sokoban` script in the **Project** panel and switch over to MonoDevelop. Find `levels array` and modify it to be as follows:

```
// Create the top array, this will store the level arrays
int [][][] levels =
{
  // Create the level array, this will store the row array
  new int [][] {
  // Create all row array, these will store column data
  new int[] {1,1,1,1,1,1,1,1},
  new int[] {1,0,0,1,0,0,0,1},
  new int[] {1,0,3,3,0,3,0,1},
  new int[] {1,0,0,1,0,1,0,1},
  new int[] {1,0,0,1,3,1,0,1},
  new int[] {1,0,0,2,2,2,2,1},
  new int[] {1,0,0,1,0,4,1,1},
  new int[] {1,1,1,1,1,1,1,1}
},
// Create a new level
new int [][] {
  new int[] {1,1,1,1,0,0,0,0},
  new int[] {1,0,0,1,1,1,1,1},
  new int[] {1,0,2,0,0,3,0,1},
  new int[] {1,0,3,0,0,2,4,1},
  new int[] {1,1,1,0,0,1,1,1},
  new int[] {0,0,1,1,1,1,0,0}
},
// Create a new level
  new int [][] {
  new int[] {1,1,1,1,1,1,1,1},
  new int[] {1,4,0,1,2,2,2,1},
  new int[] {1,0,0,3,3,0,0,1},
  new int[] {1,0,3,0,0,0,1,1},
  new int[] {1,0,0,1,1,1,1},
  new int[] {1,0,0,1},
  new int[] {1,1,1,1}
  }
};
```

The preceding code has given us two extra levels, bringing the total to three. The layout of the arrays is still very visual and you can easily see the level layout just by looking at the arrays.

Our `BuildLevel`, `CheckIfPlayerIsAttempingToMove` and `MovePlayer` methods only work on the first level at the moment, let's update them to always use the users current level. We'll have to store which level the player is currently on and use that level at all times, incrementing the value when a level is finished. As we'll want this value to persist between plays, we'll be using the `PlayerPrefs` object that Unity provides for saving player data. Before we get the value, we need to check that it is actually set and exists; otherwise we could see some odd results.

Start by declaring our variable for use at the top of the `Sokoban` script as follows:

```
int currentLevel;
```

Next, we'll need to get the value of the current level from the `PlayerPrefs` object and store it in the `Awake` method. Add the following code to the top of your `Awake` method:

```
if (PlayerPrefs.HasKey("currentLevel")) {
   currentLevel = PlayerPrefs.GetInt("currentLevel");
} else {
   currentLevel = 0;
   PlayerPrefs.SetInt("currentLevel", currentLevel);
}
```

Here we are checking if we have a value already stored in the `PlayerPrefs` object, if we do then use it, if we don't then set `currentLevel` to 0, and then save it to the `PlayerPrefs` object. To fix the methods mentioned earlier, click on **Search | Replace**. A new window will appear. Type `levels[0]` in the top box and `levels[currentLevel]` in the bottom one, and then click on **All**.

[71]

Level complete detection

It's all well and good having three levels, but without a mechanism to move between them they are useless. We are going to add a check to see if the player has finished a level, if they have then increment the level counter and load the next level in the array. We only need to do the check at the end of every move; to do so every frame would be redundant.

We'll write the following method first and then explain it:

```
// If this method returns true then we have finished the level
boolhaveFinishedLevel () {
  // Initialise the counter for how many crates are on goal
  // tiles
  int cratesOnGoalTiles = 0;
  // Loop through all the rows in the current level
  for (int i = 0; i< levels[currentLevel].Length; i++) {
    // Get the tile ID for the column and pass it the switch
    // statement
    for (int j = 0; j < levels[currentLevel][i].Length; j++) {
      switch (levels[currentLevel][i][j]) {
        case 5:
        // Do we have a match for a crate on goal
        // tile ID? If so increment the counter
        cratesOnGoalTiles++;
        break;
        default:
        break;
      }
    }
  }

  // Check if the cratesOnGoalTiles variable is the same as the
  // amountOfCrates we set when building the level
  if (amountOfCrates == cratesOnGoalTiles) {
    return true;
  } else {
    return false;
  }
}
```

In the `BuildLevel` method, whenever we instantiate `crate`, we increment the `amountOfCrates` variable. We can use this variable to check if the amount of crates on goal tiles is the same as the `amountOfCrates` variable, if it is then we know we have finished the current level. The `for` loops iterate through the current level's rows and columns, and we know that 5 in the array is a crate on a goal tile. The method returns a Boolean based on whether we have finished the level or not. Now let's add the call to the method. The logical place would be inside the `MovePlayer` method, so go ahead and add a call to the method just after the `pCol += tCol;` statement.

As the method returns `true` or `false`, we're going to use it in an `if` statement, as shown in the following code:

```
// Check if we have finished the level
if (haveFinishedLevel()) {
  Debug.Log("Finished");
}
```

The `Debug.Log` method will do for now, let's check if it's working. The solution for level one is on YouTube at http://www.youtube.com/watch?v=K5SMwAJrQM8&hd=1. Click on the play icon at the top-middle of the Unity screen and copy the sequence of moves in the video (or solve it yourself), when all the crates are on the goal tiles you'll see **Finished** in the **Console** panel.

Moving to the next level

Assuming everything went correctly, you should have seen the `Finished` text appear. Next is to load a new level which is probably going to be easier than you think. We already have all the code to build a level and add the character in our current scene. Rather than elaborately tear it down and unload the current assets, we can simply increment the `currentLevel` counter and then reload the scene; our existing code will take care of the rest. Replace the `Debug.Log` method with the following code:

```
// Check if we have finished the level
if (haveFinishedLevel()) {

  currentLevel++;
  if (currentLevel == levels.Length) {
    currentLevel = 0;
  }
  PlayerPrefs.SetInt("currentLevel", currentLevel);

  Invoke("LoadNextLevel", 1.0f);
}
```

Here, we are checking if we have finished the level with the `haveFinishedlevel` method, and then incrementing the `currentLevel` counter. The next check makes sure that it doesn't go over the amount of levels we actually have by comparing it to the `Length` of the levels array, if it does go over, we set it back to `0` to loop the level order. We then store the level in the `PlayerPrefs` object, so you can resume from that point after quitting the game. The last line is the `Invoke` method, as we don't want to load the new level at the exact moment, we finish placing the last `crate`. We can invoke a method after a delay. Here, the method to `Invoke` is named `LoadNextLevel` and the delay is `1.0f`, which means one second. Let's create the `LoadLevel` method:

```
Void LoadNextlevel () {
  Application.LoadLevel("GameScreen");
}
```

As you've seen previously, `Application.LoadLevel` just loads a new scene, and because we have set out method to use the `currentLevel` variable, we can simply reload our scene to render the next level.

Restarting our level

Sometimes things just don't go your way. In `Sokoban`, you can get yourself into a situation where it is impossible to complete the level. As this is the case, then we need the ability to restart the game. Let's map it to the `Y` button on the Ouya controller. Add the following code to the bottom of your `Update` method:

```
// Should we restart the current level?
if (OuyaInput.GetButtonDown(OuyaButton.Y, playerNumber)) {
  Application.LoadLevel("GameScreen");
}
```

Give your game a test on the Ouya, and when in the main game, click on the `Y` button. You should reset back to the start position.

Adding sounds

When you start adding sounds in to your game, it takes on a whole new dimension, you'd be surprised how a game that seems unfinished can suddenly feel almost complete just by adding some sounds effects. We're going to add a sound that will play every time a crate is moved on to a goal tile. With keeping our project tidy in mind, the first step is to create a folder that will store all our sound files.

Click on the **Create** dropdown menu in the **Project** panel. Click on **Folder** and a new folder will be created in the project panel, call the folder `Sounds`. Import the asset `crateOnGoal.mp3` from the files for this chapter to your new `Sounds` folder.

Sound in Unity requires the following three things:

- A sound to play
- A source for the sound to come from
- A listener to hear the sound

Our **Main Camera** already has an `Audio Listener` component attached to it and we have already imported our sound to play, all that's left is to add an audio source with a reference to our sound and a trigger to call it. Click on the `Sokoban` GameObject, then click on **Component | Audio | Audio Source**. You'll see in the **Inspector** panel that the new component has appeared that is **Audio Source**.

Drag your `crateOnGoal` sound effect to the **Audio Clip** section of the component; this is how **Audio Source** knows which sound to play. We also need to uncheck the **Play On Awake** box, as we only want the sound to play when a box is moved on to a goal by the player, as shown in the following screenshot:

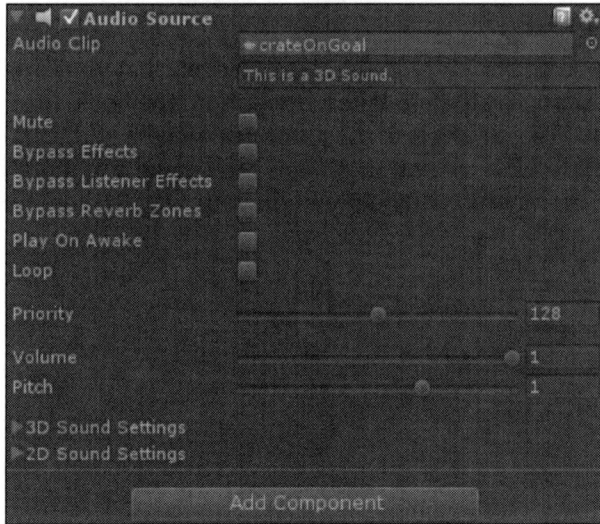

Our audio component is now configured. Go back to MonoDevelop and edit your `Sokoban` script, we need to find the appropriate place to add our sound code. The `MovePlayer` method is a good place. We need to add it when we know a move has finished, so it will be inside of the `if (movingSteps == 10) {` statement. As we want it to play only when moving a crate we'll also have to have it inside the `if (movingCrate != "") {` statement. Add the following code at the bottom of the statement, inside the closing brace:

```
if (levels[currentLevel][pRow + 2 * tRow][pCol + 2 * tCol] == 5) {
  audio.Play();
}
```

We only want to play the sound if the crate is on a goal tile, so we check that the array's index is 5, which is the number we use for a crate on a goal tile. As **Audio Source** is attached to the same GameObject as the `Sokoban` script, we can just call `audio.Play` to play the sound. Click on the play icon at the top-middle of the Unity screen and position a crate on a goal tile, you should have a cool space-style sound effect play. If not then check you dragged the sound file to the **Audio Source** component and that your sound on your test device is turned up.

Summary

The game now has some structure in the form of levels that you can complete and is easily expandable. If you wanted to take a break from the book, now would be a great time to create and add some levels to the game and maybe add some extra sound effects. All this hard work is for nothing if you can't make any money though, isn't it? *Chapter 6, Show Me the Money!*, will help you on your way to monetizing your creation.

6
Show Me the Money!

We now have a game. You could give it away for free but the Ouya also supports **In-App Purchase**. There are two types of In-App Purchase:

- **An entitlement**: This is a great way of letting players try out your game and then, if they like it, unlocking new features or levels with a one-off payment.
- **A consumable**: This is usually represented as coins, gems, or some other kind of in-game currency. They can be used, and as the name suggests, consumed.

This chapter assumes you have set up a company and entered all your tax information on the Ouya website. If not then you can only give your game away for free and you can skip this chapter.

Setting up your purchase

Before we can dive in to Unity and get started with coding, we're going to have to use the Ouya website to create our In-App Purchase. Log in to the **Ouya Developer Portal** at `https://devs.ouya.tv/developers` and click on the **Products** option from the top menu. It will take you to a screen where you need to complete the following fields:

- **Identifier**: Call it `SokobanUnlock`.
- **Name**: This is the name that the player will see. Call it `Sokoban - Full Unlock`.
- **Price**: It can be difficult choosing the price for your game. It's better to start a little higher, that way you can always offer sales at a later date. Set it to `1.99`.
- **Type**: This is going to be a one off purchase so set it to **Entitlement**.

Show Me the Money!

When you've entered all that information, click on **Create Product** and you'll be taken back to the **Products** screen.

The Ouya store will pay you when your game earns over $150, and the payments will come 30 days after the month in which the money was earned. The Ouya store takes 30% of the sale price, which is standard for the industry now.

Setting up your game

To perform any In-App Purchase, your game must also be signed with a `key.der` file. Ouya will generate this file for you after you create a listing for your game on their website.

While we're on the Ouya website, let's do that too. Go to `https://devs.ouya.tv/developers/games` and click on **Add a Game**. Add the values to the following fields:

- **Title**: `Sokoban 3D`, if this is taken use a name of your liking — currently the Ouya platform is allowing duplicate application names although this is likely to change.
- **Android package name**: `com.generic.sokoban`, if this is taken use a name of your liking. Currently the Ouya platform is allowing you to submit duplicate bundle IDs although this is also likely to change. If you do change your bundle ID then revisit *Chapter 2, Setting Up Unity and the Ouya Plugin*, and follow the steps to set up your new bundle ID in Unity.
- **OUYA exclusive**: **No** – if your app is going to only come out on Ouya then set this to **Yes**. We will be converting our game to run on Android phones, which is why we set it to **No**.
- **Expected**: The date you plan to release the game.
- **Developer permission**: **Yes** – saying **Yes** here means that Ouya will publicize the release of your game on the Ouya website.

Tick the three checkboxes and click on **Create**, you'll be taken to a screen for more information. The required fields on this page are **Description**, **Content rating**, **Support email address**, and **Website**, so fill in those fields and then click on **Save**. The **My Games** screen will appear with your new entry. One of the items alongside your entry will be **Signing Key** with a **Download** button. Download your `key.der` file and save it to (your game project folder)`\Assets\Plugins\Android\res\raw\key.der`. This will now allow you to sign your apps for release and the In-App Purchase to work.

Implementing the Ouya payment framework

The Ouya examples provide a really good stub class for your In-App Purchase needs, we'll import that in to our project as a base for the code. The file is located in the folder where you installed the Ouya Unity repository to in *Chapter 2, Setting Up Unity and the Ouya Plugin*. From inside that folder navigate to `Assets\Ouya\Examples\Scripts` and drag the `OuyaShowProducts` file in to the `Scripts` folder in our **Project** panel. Double-click on it to edit it in MonoDevelop, and have a look at the method names to become familiar with the method names that we will need to call and respond to. At the moment we're going to use the script as it is. There is some code already in the script that will build a **Graphical User Interface** (**GUI**) and display a menu system for seeing your products.

Back in Unity, open your **SetUp** scene and add a new, empty game object to it. Call it `IAP` and drag your `OuyaShowProducts` script on to it. We need to make sure that this new, empty game object persists across all scenes as well as `OuyaGameObject`, so let's create a script that we can use for both the game objects.

Create a new C# script and call it `DontDestroyOnLoad`. Edit the script as shown in the following code:

```
using UnityEngine;
using System.Collections;

public class DontDestroyOnLoad : MonoBehaviour {

    // Use this for initialization
    void Awake () {

        // Make it so this object persists
        DontDestroyOnLoad(this);
    }
}
```

Save the script and drag it on to your `IAP` game object and `OuyaGameObject`. This will make sure that they persist across all scenes. The final thing we need to do before we can see some results is to let `OuyaGameObject` know about the names of the products it will need to request information about initially. To do this, click on `OuyaGameObject` in Unity and the **Inspector** panel will show the word **Purchasables** in **Ouya Game Object (Script)**. If this isn't expanded then expand **Purchasables** and you'll see a **Size** property, change it to 1. In the **Element 0** label add `SokobanUnlock`.

Show Me the Money!

If you want to sell multiple products in the future you'll need to increase the size of the **Purchasables** array and add the names to it. With the exception of the **DEVELOPER_ID**, you can see how the **Inspector** panel should appear in the following screenshot:

Make sure Ouya is connected to the Internet and run the game on it. You will see that there is now some text and three buttons on the screen. You have to wait until the In-App Purchase system is initialized before you call anything on it. You can see the status in the top-left of the screen. When you see the **IAP is initialized** message, you're good to go. Using the mouse-like area of the Ouya controller to bring up a mouse pointer, click on the **Get Products** button and you'll see your **Sokoban Unlock** appear. Click on the **Purchase** button next to it and you'll be presented with the In-App Purchase screen for the Ouya.

 If your Ouya developer login ID is the same as the account you logged in to your Ouya with, then you won't be charged for your In-App Purchases.

How to manage your purchases

While testing your code to check if In-App Purchases works, you'll need to buy it over and over again, thankfully Ouya took this in to consideration and made it easy to manage any purchases you have made of your own products. After you have bought your In-App Purchase, and providing your Ouya developer login is the same as the account you logged in to your Ouya with, you will be able to see your purchase on the Ouya Developer website: `https://devs.ouya.tv/developers/purchases`.

Getting the list of products

As we know our In-App Purchases are now set up correctly on the website and we can start to properly implement them in our game. Double-click on the `OuyaShowProducts` script to open it in MonoDevelop and scroll to the bottom of the file. You'll see a method called `OnGUI`, when you find it comment out the whole method using `/*` and `*/`. This is a way of commenting out entire blocks of code without having to use `//` on every line.

Let's create a method that will get our products and store them in an array. At the top of our file, where the variables are defined add the following line of code:

```
bool iAPDone = false;
```

We create this Boolean as we're going to have an `if` statement that we only want to be called once. The `if` statement will need to called in the `Update` method. The method should be written as following:

```
void Update () {

  // Is the IAP engine initialized and have we NOT called
  // this code previously?
  if (OuyaSDK.isIAPInitComplete() && iAPDone == false) {

    // Make it so we don't call this code again
    iAPDone = true;

    // Create a List (like an array) to store our products
    List<OuyaSDK.Purchasable> productIdentifierList =
      new List<OuyaSDK.Purchasable>();

    // Loop through all the purchasables specified in the
    // OuyaGameObject
    foreach (string productId in
      OuyaGameObject.Singleton.Purchasables)
    {
      // Add the product name to the List
      productIdentifierList.Add(
        new OuyaSDK.Purchasable(productId));
    }

    // Initiate a request to get the reciepts.
    // This will be used to check if we have already bought
    // any of these items
    OuyaSDK.requestReceiptList();

    // Get the information about the products in the List
    OuyaSDK.requestProductList(productIdentifierList);
  }
}
```

Comments have been left in the code to provide a line by line explanation but the overview is:

- Has the In-App Purchase engine initialized and not been called before
- Set a Boolean so this code won't be called again
- Create `List` to store any products we need to get information on
- Loop through the `Purchasables` array in `OuyaGameObject`
- Add any `Purchasables` to `List`
- Get the list of receipts to see if any of the products have already been bought
- Get information about all the products listed in `productIdentifierList`

Limiting your levels

If you're just dealing with an entitlement In-App Purchase then it's easier to build the game completely and then add in the In-App Purchase code afterwards. We've added three levels to our game already so that's a good place to start. We're going to limit it so there is only one level until you pay to unlock them all. Double-click on your `Sokoban` script to open it in MonoDevelop and, at the top of the script where the variables are defined, add the following line of code:

```
int trialLevelAmount = 1;
```

We now need to modify our `MovePlayer` method. Scroll to the bottom of the method and find the `if (haveFinishedLevel())` condition. We need to edit it as shown in the following code:

```
if (haveFinishedLevel()) {

  currentLevel++;

  if ((PlayerPrefs.HasKey("purchased") && currentLevel <
    levels.Length) || currentLevel < trialLevelAmount) {
    Invoke("LoadNextLevel", 1.0f);
  } else {
    currentLevel = 0;
    Invoke("LoadTitleScreen", 1.0f);
  }

  PlayerPrefs.SetInt("currentLevel", currentLevel);
}
```

You can see that the `if` statement that we perform now is slightly different. We check if the player has purchased the full unlock and whether the current level is less than the full array of levels, if the game has not been purchased we only check if the current level is less than the trial-level amount. This means that the player will be sent back to the title screen when they have finished all the levels if they have bought the game, or when they finish the first level if they haven't bought it.

We have called a new method, `LoadTitleScreen`, which we also need to create. It's very simple, add the following code:

```
void LoadTitleScreen () {
   Application.LoadLevel("TitleScreen");
}
```

Unlocking levels for people who have paid

If the player has already paid for the unlockable levels we need to make sure they are always available. We'll achieve this by using two systems; first we'll check if `int` has been set in `PlayerPrefs`. Secondly, we'll download the receipts and see if this product has been purchased previously. We have to do both as if the game is deleted from the user's Ouya then the `PlayerPrefs` information will be deleted. You'll remember earlier that in `OuyaShowProducts` we added the `Update` method and, in there, called the `OuyaSDK.requestReceiptList` method. When the receipts come down from the server, `OuyaGetReceiptsOnSuccess` is called. There was already a stub method in place so let's expand on it:

```
public void OuyaGetReceiptsOnSuccess(List<OuyaSDK.Receipt>
   receipts)
{
   // Clear the current receipts List
   m_receipts.Clear();
   
   // Loop through all the receipts and verify we have one
   // with our SokobanUnlock identifier in
   foreach (OuyaSDK.Receipt receipt in receipts)
   {
      if (receipt.getIdentifier() == "SokobanUnlock") {
      
         // If we have previously purchased the
         // SokobanUnlock then store it in the PlayerPrefs
         PlayerPrefs.SetInt("purchased", 1);
      }
      m_receipts.Add(receipt);
   }
}
```

The method will pass a list of receipts, all we need to do is loop through all the receipts and see if any of them have the identifier of `SokobanUnlock`. If they do, then we know that the user has purchased the game and we can set `int` in `PlayerPrefs`.

Buying your product

The majority of the hard work has already been done by this point; we have our trial-level amount code, we have our receipt checking, the only thing left to do is to create a mechanism to actually buy the game. As we now drop the game back to the title screen when we finish the demo or the full game, the title screen is a perfect place to offer the game for sale. It's good **User Experience (UX)** to not offer the purchase to people who have already bought the game. The tasks are to add a new menu items to the title screen, call the buy method if that item is selected, and hide the item if the game has already been purchased. Let's start with the first of those.

Adding a new menu item

In Unity, double-click on your **TitleScreen** scene to edit it. We're going to add some more text just like we did earlier to navigate to **GameObject | Create Other | 3D Text**. Change the name of the new game object to `Purchase Instructions`. Click and drag the new text in to the Main Camera's game object and then change the following settings:

- Set **Position** to **X**: `0` **Y**: `-5` **Z**: `50`
- Set **Text** to `Press A to Purchase`
- Set **Anchor** to **middle center**
- Set **Font Size** to `50`

You will also have to edit the `Play Instructions` game object to get it positioned correctly with the new menu entry:

- Set the **Y** of the `Play Instructions` game object to `5`

Test your game inside Unity and your title screen should look like the following screenshot:

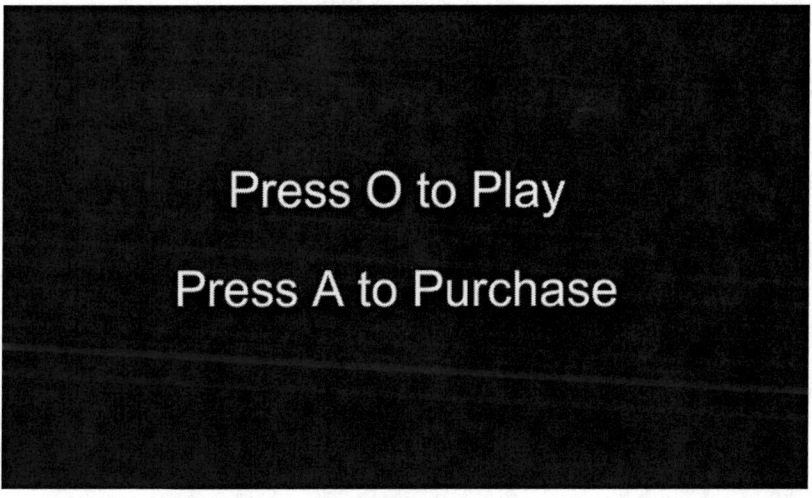

The buy method

We now need to create a method that is going to purchase our product upon pressing the A button on the Ouya controller, the best place for this is within our `OuyaShowProducts` script. Create a new method in the script called `BuyFullGame` and add the following code:

```
public void BuyFullGame () {
   if (PlayerPrefs.HasKey("purchased")) {
      // The game has already been brought, don't continue
      return;
   }

   foreach (OuyaSDK.Product product in m_products)
   {
      // Is this the product we want to buy?
      if (product.getIdentifier() == "SokobanUnlock") {
         OuyaSDK.requestPurchase(product.getIdentifier());
      }
   }
}
```

First we check that we haven't already bought the game, obviously we don't want to be able to purchase it twice. After that we loop through all the objects that we stored in our `m_products` list earlier when we called `OuyaSDK.requestProductList`. The `m_products` list is created for you by the code in the `OuyaShowProducts` script. This will then bring up the Ouya purchase dialog that you saw earlier and, upon clicking on **PURCHASE**, will trigger the `OuyaPurchaseOnSuccess` method.

To hook up the A button, we need to edit our `ControlsTitleScreen` script. Double-click on the `ControlsTitleScreen` script to edit it in MonoDevelop and go to the `Update` method. We're going to add an `else` condition to the `if` statement:

```
if (Input.GetKeyDown(KeyCode.Space) ||
  OuyaInput.GetButtonDown(OuyaButton.O, player)){
    Application.LoadLevel("GameScreen");
} else if (OuyaInput.GetButtonDown(OuyaButton.A, player)) {

    GameObject iap = GameObject.Find("IAP");
    OuyaShowProducts showProductsScript =
      iap.GetComponent<OuyaShowProducts>();
    showProductsScript.BuyFullGame();
}
```

Here we have added a check for the A button, and if that is pressed, we find the `IAP` game object. As previously stated, the `Find` operation is expensive, but as this won't be called often it's fine to use in this instance. Once we have found it we need to get a reference to the `OuyaShowProducts` script that's attached to it, that's what the `GetComponent` method achieves. As we made our `BuyFullGame` method public, it means we call it from this script.

Once a purchase has been successful the `OuyaPurchaseOnSuccess` method will be called. Modify the method as shown in the following code:

```
public void OuyaPurchaseOnSuccess(OuyaSDK.Product product)
{
    PlayerPrefs.SetInt("purchased", 1);

    Application.LoadLevel("TitleScreen");

    // Once the purchase is complete get a list of all receipts
    OuyaSDK.requestReceiptList();
}
```

You can see that on a successful purchase we now store a value in `PlayerPrefs`, reload the **TitleScreen** scene, and request the receipt list. This last step is done for completeness. You'll see why we reload the scene in out next section.

Hiding menu items

We've got a functioning method to buy our level now but the message when you load the game still has the option to buy it. We need to detect if the app has already been purchased and hide the purchase option if it has. The first step for this is to delete your purchases in case you have already purchased the product, this can be done at `https://devs.ouya.tv/developers/purchases`.

Create a new script in the `Scripts` folder and call it `HideIfPurchased`. Click and drag the script on to our `Purchase Instructions` game object and then double-click on the file to edit it in MonoDevelop. Edit the `Start` method as shown in the following code:

```
void Start () {
  if (PlayerPrefs.HasKey("purchased")) {
    this.transform.gameObject.SetActive(false);
  }
}
```

We simply check if we have a value for `purchased` in our `PlayerPrefs`, if we do then we hide the game object. If you recall, we set `purchased` to `1` and reload the **TitleScreen** scene when `OuyaPurchaseOnSuccess` gets called.

Submitting your game

We're almost ready to submit our game but we just need to do one final thing: replace the icon. The default Ouya icon is at (your game project folder)`\Assets\Plugins\Android\res\drawable-xhdpi\ouya_icon.png` and it's a 732 x 412 pixels PNG file. Replace it with the icon of your choice and then go to the build settings by navigating to **File | Build Settings...** and click on **Build** and type a name for the file in the text field, and then click on **Save**.

Now that's saved we need to go back to the **My Games** page on the Ouya website and click on **Edit**. Add some screenshots; they need to be 1280 pixels wide by 720 pixels high and you need a minimum of three; can submit up to nine. Scroll down to the bottom and click on **Upload APK**, then follow the on-screen instructions, once the upload is complete click on **Save**. This will take you back to the **My Games** page where you'll most likely see that Ouya are still verifying your APK. Give it a few minutes and then refresh the page, the warnings should have disappeared.

Finally, click on **Submit for review**. The status should change to **Submitted** and you're done! The review process normally takes a few days but that can go up or down depending how busy they are.

Summary

Our game is now complete! Pour yourself a drink of your choice and give your game a play. It's pretty sweet, huh? We have successfully implemented an entitlement In-App Purchase but what about the other type mentioned at the start of this chapter? You can read all the Ouya documentation on In-App Purchases at `https://devs.ouya.tv/developers/docs/purchasing`. Next, let's look at what it takes to get our app running on an Android phone or tablet.

7
Building Cross-platform Games

One of Unity's strongest features is its write-once, publish-everywhere functionality. Our game isn't quite ready for that, but with very little work, we'll have it running on Android devices.

The Ouya controller functionality we added earlier already supports PS3 controllers paired to an Android device but we should add some touch screen controls too.

Although we're focusing on Android, the game will run on any device that Unity supports, but the setup of all those development environments requires a book in itself.

 This chapter explains how to get the game running on Android. To test your code, you will need an Android phone or tablet. If you don't have one, you won't be able to test the code, but it is still beneficial to read the chapter.

Platform Dependent Compilation

Unity includes a feature called **Platform Dependent Compilation**. It consists of some preprocessor directives that let you partition your scripts to compile and execute sections of code for one of the supported platforms. This functionality is also supported within Editor, so you can compile the code specifically for your mobile or console and test it in Editor.

This is useful if you're branching code for things, such as In-App Purchase or control mechanisms. To use the Platform Dependent Compilation feature, you use the pound or hash symbol, as shown in the following code:

```
void Start () {

   #if UNITY_EDITOR
     Debug.Log("Unity Editor");
   #endif

   #if UNITY_ANDROID
     Debug.Log("Android");
   #endif

   #if UNITY_IPHONE
     Debug.Log("iPhone");
   #endif

   #if UNITY_STANDALONE_OSX
     Debug.Log("Stand Alone OSX");
   #endif

   #if UNITY_STANDALONE_WIN
     Debug.Log("Stand Alone Windows");
   #endif
}
```

While this is brilliant for coding between platforms, it doesn't actually help in our example. The Ouya and an Android phone might seem different, but they both run on the Android operating system, even though the Ouya does a good job at hiding that. It means our platform-dependent compilation is going to trigger for Android in both scenarios. Thankfully, the Ouya SDK thought of this and provided a method we can call instead. The method is `OuyaSDK.IsOUYA()` and it is called as shown in the following code:

```
if (OuyaSDK.IsOUYA()) {

   // Remove the In-App Purchase here as
   // it's not needed for mobile
}
```

Changing the TitleScreen scene

Currently our title screen has **Press O to Play** and **Press A to Purchase** on it, neither of these will apply to the Android version of the game, so let's add something a little more fitting. How about `Tap to Start`? We're going to have three 3D text GameObjects on our screen and we'll need to toggle the visibility depending on if we are or are not on Ouya. The best way to do this is with a simple script. Create a new C# script and call it `ToggleVisibilityForOuya`. At the top of the script, where variables are defined, add the following code:

```
public bool visibleIfOuya;
```

Change the `Start` method to an `Awake` method and change it to the following code:

```
void Awake () {
  if (OuyaSDK.IsOUYA()) {
    this.gameObject.SetActive(visibleIfOuya);
  } else if (!OuyaSDK.IsOUYA()) {
    this.gameObject.SetActive(!visibleIfOuya);
  }
}
```

The preceding code will make sure that when we run on the Ouya with the `visibleIfOuya` script, a Boolean set will show up and if we're not running on the Ouya then the opposite will show up. Now perform the following steps:

1. Save your script and go back to Unity. Rather than creating a new 3D text and setting all the parameters again, we can duplicate one of the existing ones. Make sure you're editing the **TitleScreen** scene, click on the **Play Instructions** GameObject in the **Hierarchy** panel, and then click on **Edit | Duplicate**.

2. Now you'll have two copies of **Play Instructions**, change the name of one of them to `Tap to Play`.

3. While it is selected, move over to the **Inspector** panel and change the position of **Transform** to Y to 0, and the text of **Text Mesh** to `Tap to Play`.

4. Click and drag your `ToggleVisibilityForOuya` script onto all three of the 3D text GameObjects, namely **Play Instructions**, **Purchase Instructions**, and **Tap to Play**.

5. Click on **Play Instructions** and, in the **Inspector** panel, tick the **Visible If Ouya** box.

6. Click on **Purchase Instructions**, and in the **Inspector** panel, tick the **Visible If Ouya** box.

7. Click on **Tap to Play**, and in the **Inspector** panel, make sure the tick box is unticked.

Run the game on your Android device and the title screen should just have **Tap to Play** on. Let's add some code to make that actually happen. Double-click on your `ControlsTitleScreen` script to edit it in MonoDevelop and change the `Update` method as follows:

```
void Update () {

  #if UNITY_ANDROID
  if (OuyaSDK.IsOUYA ()) {
    // Update the controllers here for best results
    OuyaInput.UpdateControllers();

    if (Input.GetKeyDown(KeyCode.Space) ||
      OuyaInput.GetButtonDown(OuyaButton.O, player)) {
      Application.LoadLevel("GameScreen");
    } else
    if (OuyaInput.GetButtonDown(OuyaButton.A, player)) {

      GameObject iap = GameObject.Find("IAP");
      OuyaShowProducts showProductsScript =
        iap.GetComponent<OuyaShowProducts>();
      showProductsScript.BuyFullGame();
    }
  } else {
    if (Input.touchCount >= 1) {
      Application.LoadLevel("GameScreen");
    }
  }
  #endif
}
```

You can see that we now wrapped all the code in a platform-dependent compilation block, so it will only trigger on Android devices, this means we can implement different control systems for different platforms. We then check if we are running on the Ouya or an Android phone with OuyaSDK.IsOUYA. If it returns false we just check for a tap anywhere on the screen to start the game.

Test the game on your Android device now to verify it's all working as it should for you.

Removing In-App Purchases

The Ouya SDK makes In-App Purchase relatively simple; it integrates nicely with Unity out of the box. Android, on the other hand, can be a pain to integrate with In-App Purchase inside Unity unless you use a plugin from the **Asset Store**. For this reason, we'll be modifying our Android game to not use In-App Purchase and instead make it work like a full game purchased from one of the many Android app stores.

As we already have the code for giving the player all the levels when we have purchased the game on the Ouya, the simplest way to remove the In-App Purchase requirement would be to set the purchased int in PlayerPrefs when the game starts.

Double-click on your Sokoban script, as we're going to modify our Awake method. Add the following code to the top of it:

```
#if UNITY_ANDROID
if (OuyaSDK.IsOUYA () == false){
  PlayerPrefs.SetInt("purchased", 1);
}
#endif
```

The preceding code is checking if we are on Android but not on Ouya, and if that condition is met then we set the purchased int to 1. We've already tested the code when the game was purchased, so we know this code will work too.

Mobile controls

We're going to keep our controls really simple for this demo, there won't be a virtual joystick or button in sight. As we only need three functions, namely `left`, `forward`, and `right`, we'll be breaking the screen up in to three sections and using the left section for turning left, the center section for forward, and the right section for turning right. The following is a screenshot of the game with the control areas overlaid for illustration purposes:

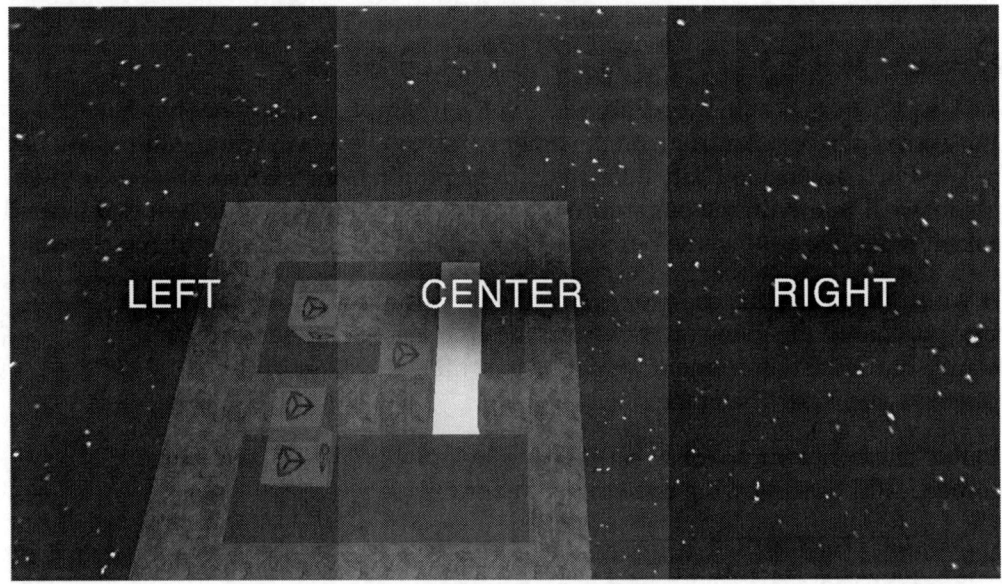

We already have our control script for the game, `Sokoban`, so go ahead and double-click on it to edit it in MonoDevelop.

We're going to create a new method that will return `true` or `false` when we pass it in a string for the control direction we want to check. It should only return `true` if the tap has just happened, and not keep returning `true` if the user holds his finger on the screen. The method is as follows:

```
// Check if an area of the screen has been
// touched for the very first time
bool FirstTouchForControlType(string controlType) {

    // Is there only one press?
    if (Input.touchCount == 1) {

        // Get the touch out of the touches
        // array as a touch object
```

```
      Touch touch = Input.touches[0];

    // Has the touch just started?
    if (touch.phase == TouchPhase.Began) {

      // Get the screen sections
      float screenSectionLeft = Screen.width / 3;
      float screenSectionCenter = screenSectionLeft +
        Screen.width / 3;
      float screenSectionRight = Screen.width;

      // Check the passed control type
      if (controlType == "left") {

        // Have we hit the left section?
        if (touch.position.x <= screenSectionLeft) {
          return true;
        } else {
          return false;
        }
      } else if (controlType == "forward") {

      // Have we hit the forward section?
      if (touch.position.x >= screenSectionLeft &&
        touch.position.x <= screenSectionCenter) {
        return true;
      } else {
        return false;
      }
    } else if (controlType == "right") {

      // Have we hit the right section?
      if (touch.position.x >= screenSectionCenter &&
        touch.position.x <= screenSectionRight) {
        return true;
      } else {
        return false;
      }
    }
  }
}

  return false;
}
```

Let's break that code down as there's quite a large amount. Firstly, we check that there is only one finger on the screen, we then get the touch at index 0 and store it in to a variable named `touch`. As we only want the method to return `true` when the finger is first placed, we have to check the `touch.phase` value and make sure it's the same as `TouchPhase.Began`. After that we break the screen down into three sections, on Android the screen sizes can be variable, so it's best that this is done in code to allow for the variation. We pass in the methods to check whether `left`, `forward`, or `right` have been clicked, so the next check is the value of that string, from there on the code is self-explanatory.

Now that we have the method in place, we need to modify our movement code, it's in the same file so find the method named `CheckIfPlayerIsAttempingToMove` and find the following code line:

```
if (Input.GetKeyDown (KeyCode.UpArrow) ||
   OuyaInput.GetButtonDown(OuyaButton.DU, playerNumber)) {
```

We're going to modify it to be the following code:

```
if (Input.GetKeyDown (KeyCode.UpArrow) ||
   OuyaInput.GetButtonDown(OuyaButton.DU, playerNumber) ||
     FirstTouchForControlType("forward")) {
```

You see we've just added another check to the conditional with the OR operator, we call our method and pass in a string of `"forward"`. Do the same for `left` and `right`.

That's it! Give the game a test and try out the new `control` method. It is pretty impressive that the game now works in the editor, on the Ouya and on Android!

Summary

Unity will output to iOS, OS X, Android, Windows Phone 8, Windows 8, Blackberry 10, and many other platforms. Organization of your code and project is paramount; otherwise things will get very messy very quickly. Why don't you try making this game work on some other platforms? The best way to learn is through experimenting and performing, so what are you waiting for? If you do get stuck, the forums at `http://forum.unity3d.com` are really helpful. Hopefully you feel comfortable with the basics of programming on Unity for Ouya now and I look forward to see all the cool new things you come up with. This demo alone could be expanded to have hundreds of levels, more sounds, and some better graphical effects.

My Twitter username is `@Gary_BBGames` and I'm happy to answer any questions or help out in any way possible if you get stuck. If you create any apps or games, do let me know and I'll help promote them for you.

Thank you for taking the time to go through this book and remember, it's all new territory again and anything can be a success!

Index

A

Acorn Electron 7
Activision 7
Android NDK
  about 15
  setting up 17
  URL 17
Android operating system
  history 11
Android SDK
  installing 15
  setting up 16, 17
  URL 15
Angry Birds 12
array
  about 42
  multidimensional array 42, 43
  three-dimensional array 42
  two-dimensional array 42
Asset Store 93
Atari 6
Atari 2600 6
Atari ST 8
Awake method 60, 91, 93

B

background
  adding 68, 69
BBC Micro 7
Beginners All-purpose Symbolic
      Instruction Code (BASIC) 8
Boo 29
BuildLevel method 44-49, 62, 73

bundle identifier 23
BuyFullGame method 85, 86

C

C# 29, 30
cellular games
  history 10
character
  animating 60-63
character movement
  making 52-59
character movement, making
  Ouya controller support 59
chipping 9
Commodore 64 7
Commodore Amiga 8
Computer Space 5
consumable In-App Purchase 77

D

Debug.Log method 73
dynamic typing 30

E

entitlement In-App Purchase 77
extra level
  adding 70, 71

F

for loop 46

G

Game Boy 10
GitHub 21
  URL 21
Grand Theft Auto IV 9
Graphical User Interface (GUI) 33, 79

H

home computers
  history 7, 8

I

In-App Purchase 77
  managing 80
  removing 93
  setting up 77, 78
In-App Purchase, types
  consumable 77
  entitlement 77
indie games
  current situation 12
indie gaming industry
  history 9
installation
  Android SDK 15
  Java 16
Instantiate method 46
iPhone
  history 10
iPhone 3G phone 11
iPod Touch device 10

J

Java
  installing 16
  URL 16
Java Development Kit (JDK) 15
Java JDK 15

K

key.der file 78
Kickstarter 12

L

level
  creating 41
  limiting 82
  restarting 74
  unlocking 83
level completion
  detecting 72, 73
level, creating
  array 42, 43
  BuildLevel method 44-47

M

Mac computer
  Ouya, connecting 20
Main Camera movement
  making 49-51
materials 42
menu item
  adding 84
  hiding 87
Minecraft 12
mobile controls 94, 96
MonoDevelop 33-35
MovePlayer method 58, 73
multidimensional array 42, 43

N

Native Development Kit (NDK) 15
Net Yaroze 9
next level
  moving 73
N-Gage 10
Nintendo Entertainment System (NES) 7

O

ODK
  about 15, 21
  URL 21
Ouya
  about 12
  connecting, to Mac computer 20
  connecting, to Windows computer 18, 20

release 13
Ouya controller support 38, 40, 59
Ouya Developer Portal
 about 77
 URL 77
Ouya Development Kit. *See* **ODK**
Ouya Panel
 setting up 24-26
Ouya payment framework
 implementing 79, 80
 In-App Purchase, managing 80
 level, limiting 82
 level, unlocking 83
 product, buying 84
 product list, getting 81, 82
Ouya required prefabs 26
Ouya Unity plugin
 about 21
 URL 21
Ouya website
 Unity project, setting up 78

P

Platform Dependent Compilation
 about 90
 TitleScreen scene, changing 91, 93
PlayStation 9
Pong 6
prefab
 about 41
 creating 41
 texturing 65, 66
product
 buying 84
product, buying
 BuyFullGame method 85, 86
 menu item, adding 84
 menu item, hiding 87
product list
 getting 81, 82
Python 29

R

Read Only Memory (ROM) 7
RotatePlayer method 59

S

scenes
 advancing 37
 Ouya controller support 38, 40
 progression 36
 setting up 32
 TitleScreen menu 36
scripts 33-35
SDK 9
SDK Manager 16
Shadow of the Beast 8
Sinclair ZX Spectrum 7
Snake! 10
Software Development Kit. *See* **SDK**
Sokoban 15, 30
sounds
 adding 74, 76
Space Invaders 6
Square Enix 13
Start method 35, 37, 39, 91
switch statement 46

T

TextEdit 20
three-dimensional array 42
TitleScreen scene
 changing 91, 93
TurboSquid 60
two-dimensional array 42

U

Unity
 feature 29
Unity Asset Store 60
Unity project
 about 22
 application, compiling 26, 27
 background, adding 68, 69
 building 26, 27
 bundle identifier 23
 character, animating 60-63
 character movement, making 52-59
 executing 26, 27
 extra level, adding 70, 71

level completion, detecting 72, 73
level, creating 41
level, restarting 74
Main Camera movement, making 49-51
materials 42
next level, moving 73
Ouya Panel, setting up 24-26
Ouya required prefabs 26
prefab 41
scenes, progression 36
scenes, setting up 32
setting up 78
sounds, adding 74, 76
structure 30, 32
submitting 87

UnityScript 30
Update method 35, 39, 55, 56, 60, 92
User Experience (UX) 84

V

video game industry
history 5, 6
market crash 6
recovery 6, 7
video games
advancement 9

W

Windows computer
Ouya, connecting 18, 20
Windows Mobile 10

Thank you for buying
Ouya Unity Game Development

About Packt Publishing

Packt, pronounced 'packed', published its first book "*Mastering phpMyAdmin for Effective MySQL Management*" in April 2004 and subsequently continued to specialize in publishing highly focused books on specific technologies and solutions.

Our books and publications share the experiences of your fellow IT professionals in adapting and customizing today's systems, applications, and frameworks. Our solution based books give you the knowledge and power to customize the software and technologies you're using to get the job done. Packt books are more specific and less general than the IT books you have seen in the past. Our unique business model allows us to bring you more focused information, giving you more of what you need to know, and less of what you don't.

Packt is a modern, yet unique publishing company, which focuses on producing quality, cutting-edge books for communities of developers, administrators, and newbies alike. For more information, please visit our website: www.packtpub.com.

About Packt Open Source

In 2010, Packt launched two new brands, Packt Open Source and Packt Enterprise, in order to continue its focus on specialization. This book is part of the Packt Open Source brand, home to books published on software built around Open Source licences, and offering information to anybody from advanced developers to budding web designers. The Open Source brand also runs Packt's Open Source Royalty Scheme, by which Packt gives a royalty to each Open Source project about whose software a book is sold.

Writing for Packt

We welcome all inquiries from people who are interested in authoring. Book proposals should be sent to author@packtpub.com. If your book idea is still at an early stage and you would like to discuss it first before writing a formal book proposal, contact us; one of our commissioning editors will get in touch with you.

We're not just looking for published authors; if you have strong technical skills but no writing experience, our experienced editors can help you develop a writing career, or simply get some additional reward for your expertise.

Getting Started with Unity

ISBN: 978-1-84969-584-8   Paperback: 170 pages

Learn how to use Unity by creating your very own "Outbreak" survival game while developing your essential skills

1. Use basic AI techniques to bring your game to life

2. Learn how to use Mecanim; create states and manage them through scripting

3. Use scripting to manage the graphical interface, collisions, animations, persistent data, or transitions between scenes

jQuery Game Development Essentials

ISBN: 978-1-84969-506-0   Paperback: 244 pages

Learn how to make fun and addictive multi-platform games using jQuery

1. Discover how you can create a fantastic RPG, arcade game, or platformer using jQuery

2. Learn how you can integrate your game with various social networks, creating multiplayer experiences and also ensuring compatibility with mobile devices

3. Create your very own framework, harnessing the very best design patterns and proven techniques along the way

Please check www.PacktPub.com for information on our titles

AndEngine for Android Game Development Cookbook

ISBN: 978-1-84951--898-7　　　Paperback: 380 pages

Over 70 highly effective recipes with real-world exmples to get to grips with the powerful capabilities of AndEngine and GLES 2

1. Step by step detailed instructions and information on a number of AndEngine functions, including illustrations and diagrams for added support and results

2. Learn all about the various aspects of AndEngine with prime and practical examples, useful for bringing your ideas to life

3. Improve the performance of past and future game projects with a collection of useful optimization tips

HTML5 Game Development with ImpactJS

ISBN: 978-1-84969-456-8　　　Paperback: 304 pages

A step-by-step guide to developing your own 2D games

1. A practical hands-on approach to teach you how to build your own game from scratch

2. Learn to incorporate game physics

3. How to monetize and deploy to the web and mobile platforms

Please check www.PacktPub.com for information on our titles

CPSIA information can be obtained at www.ICGtesting.com
Printed in the USA
BVOW06s1150131113

336206BV00005B/142/P